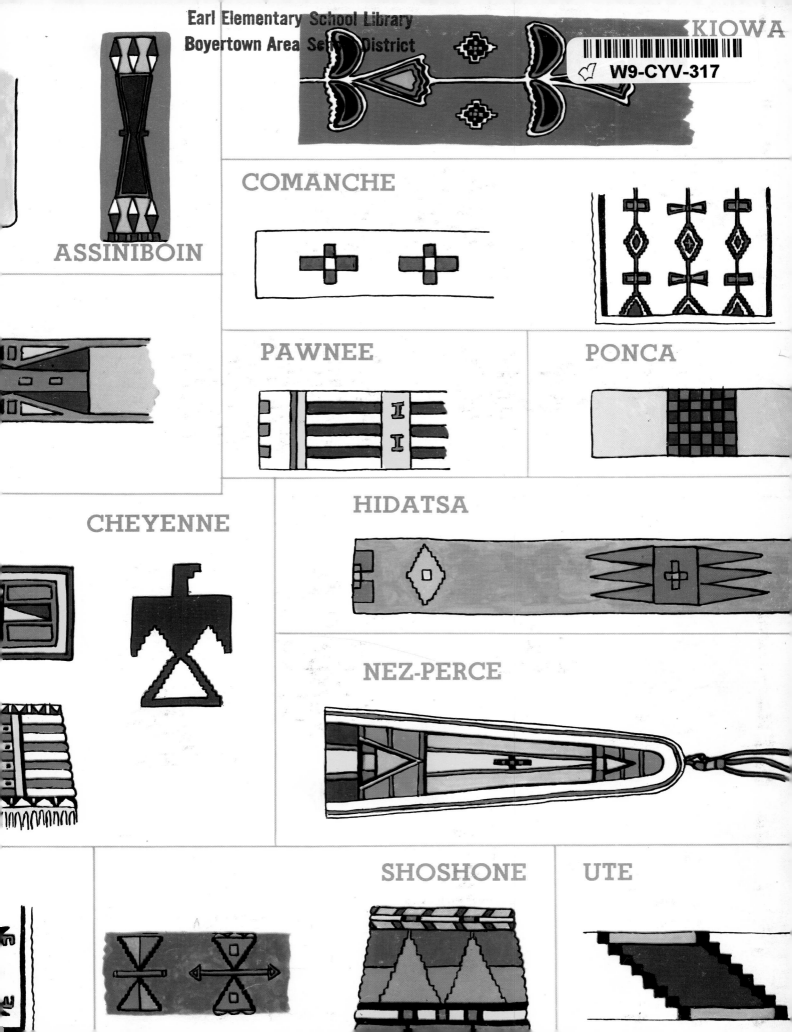

KIOWA

W9-CYV-317

ASSINIBOIN

COMANCHE

PAWNEE

PONCA

CHEYENNE

HIDATSA

NEZ-PERCE

SHOSHONE

UTE

INDIAN SIGNS AND SIGNALS

BY GEORGE FRONVAL AND DANIEL DUBOIS

middle

eternity

hunger

war

■S STERLING PUBLISHING CO., INC. NEW YORK

Oak Tree Press Co., Ltd. London & Sydney

Translated by E. W. Egan
Photographs by George C. Hight
Illustrations by Jean Marcellin
Period paintings by George Catlin

Also of Interest

The Native Americans: NAVAJOS

Third Printing, 1981

Copyright © 1978 by Sterling Publishing Co., Inc.
Two Park Avenue, New York, N.Y. 10016
Distributed in Australia by Oak Tree Press Co., Ltd.
P.O. Box J34, Brickfield Hill, Sydney 2000, N.S.W.
Distributed in the United Kingdom by Oak Tree Press Ltd. U.K.
Available in Canada from Oak Tree Press Ltd.
% Canadian Manda Group, 215 Lakeshore Boulevard East
Toronto, Ontario M5A 3W9
Manufactured in the United States of America
All rights reserved

The original edition of this book was published in France
under the title, "Les Signes Mystérieux des Peaux-Rouges,"
© 1976 by Éditions Fernand Nathan, Paris.

Library of Congress Catalog Card No.: 78-57792
Sterling ISBN 0-8069-2720-8 Trade
                          2721-6 Library
Oak Tree 7061-2600-9

Contents

Introduction

THE breeze was cool and gentle. It had finally stopped snowing. For two hours, swiftly gliding over the soft, thick snow, Black Bear had been tracking a huge deer—a fine, powerful stag. He had fatally wounded it in the flank with an arrow. The animal was proceeding with difficulty since it was losing blood heavily. The stag's halts, becoming more and more frequent, showed the man that the shadow of death was upon the beast. In a clearing ahead, the hunter spotted the stag, dying, sprawled upon the snow, which was red with blood. The creature was in its death agony, making its final gasps. Then nothing but silence.

Black Bear felt his heart jump. At last he was going to bring fresh meat home to his family, a rare event during the endless winter months. Greedily, he plunged his knife into the still warm entrails of the stag. Suddenly a stranger with a threatening look appeared.

Black Bear stood up and clutched his weapon in his icy fingers: friend or enemy? Then he made a quick movement with his hand that meant "Who are you?"

Without hesitation, the stranger replied with a tap of his right index finger on his left index finger: "Finger Cutter," or Cheyenne.

Reassured, Black Bear, with his right hand held flat against his throat, signalled his identity—"Throat Cutter," or Sioux—followed by the sign for *Friend*.

On this occasion, there would be no fight, since the Sioux and the Cheyenne were allies.

This is how, during the last century, two Indians could identify themselves during a chance encounter—by sign language, the Esperanto of the Plains Indians.

This language was used mainly by the nomadic tribes of the Great Plains, the land bounded by the Mississippi on the east and the Rocky Mountains on the west. The land of the famous mounted hunters of bison, the Plains Indians: Sioux, Cheyenne, Blackfoot, Kiowa. These tribes, a mosaic of diverse peoples who had arrived in North America in waves, often from faraway places, had no common symbol of Indian unity except this ingenious sign language (similar to deaf-and-dumb signals), the key to inter-tribal relations.

How else could these very different tribes, speaking different languages, moving about in pursuit of the bison, understand each other? These tribes spoke numerous dialects belonging to six different language families, each dialect having a sizeable vocabulary and an often complicated grammar.

Sign language appears to have evolved in the same way as spoken language, progressing gradually from the representational to the symbolic, from the picture to the symbol, but still remaining primarily representational or ideographic. The symbol usually had a clear connection with the thing it stood for: the form of an object, the movement of an action, the placement of this or that. Most

5

Jamie and Loretta Noble, Kiowa Indians, dressed in their traditional costumes, and George C. Hight before taking pictures of sign language used to illustrate this book.

Clarice Aitson, daughter of Marland. Indian name: Mah-tawn-kee-ah (daughter who is growing up).

Above: George Fronval admires beaded belts shown to him by his Indian friends Jamie and Loretta Noble. Below: Marland Aitson, Kiowa chief and distinguished scholar. Aitson is the anglicized form of A-tsan-hol, which means "warrior who killed an enemy by tricking him."

Above: Patty Aitson, sister of Clarice. Indian name: A-ho, her great grandmother's name also. (Exact meaning unknown.) Below: Bobby Goodaladdle, Kiowa.

of the signs were made at chest level, with both hands, but preferably the right, the left serving mainly as an auxiliary. Since certain signs were very similar to others, a good understanding of the language demanded close attention and considerable skill, especially when the rhythm of the "conversation"—that is, the succession of signs—was rapid.

The signs in common use—*me, you, up, down, come,* and so forth—were intuitive and natural, and many had a universal appeal. The act of placing a finger vertically against the lips, for example, means throughout the world that silence is desired.

Sign language was a very rich means of communication. It could be just as rapid and understandable as the spoken language in describing the ordinary circumstances of life. The most expert users of it were the Western Sioux—the Teton-Dakota—and the Crow and Kiowa, the latter no doubt the inventors of the language.

These mimed conversations, which often went on for hours, were veritable poems expressed in motion. A film made by Thomas A. Edison in 1898 includes a sign language sequence between the famous scout, Buffalo Bill, and his Sioux friend, Chief Iron Tail. Thus we can still witness in our own time, to our wonderment, a symphony of gestures that are both graceful and understandable and

which succeed one another with a rapid rhythm, giving an impression of true poetry—the poetry of the signalled word. What virtuosity is displayed in this historic film, executed by such remarkable hands.

During powwows, the chiefs used this sign language, especially to hold the attention of their listeners, who had to follow their most subtle gestures in order to be able to answer. This language was also indispensable on the warpath, where the success of a given manoeuvre depended on silence, and during the bison hunt, enabling different tribes keeping close to the herd to communicate with each other.

The first whites to use it were evidently the trappers known as Mountain Men, the missionaries, and scouts— the men who served as guides and interpreters for the army. The first writer of a complete book on the subject (*White Hat*) was Captain W. P. Clark, the officer who accepted the surrender of Little Wolf and his unfortunate Northern Cheyenne on the morning of March 25, 1879, near Box Elder Creek in Colorado.

George Fronval, a leading authority on the West, made a special trip to the United States from his native France to take the splendid color photographs in this book. His Indian friends of the Kiowa tribe agreed to pose for him, executing the signs used by their noble ancestors.

DANIEL DUBOIS

George Fronval and his Kiowa friends.

United States 5-cent piece, with the likeness of the Sioux chief, Iron Tail.

one

Sign Language

The text that follows describes the non-verbal way of communicating by means of sign language used by the Plains Indians. It includes more than 800 signs still in use, backed up by hundreds of original photographs.

The signs have been grouped under a number of major headings—Counting, Daily Life, Animals, On the Trail, etc. However, all entries appear in the index in alphabetical order for ready reference.

Counting

two

three

four

five

to Count The Indians usually count to ten by starting with the right hand closed, palm turned to the person being addressed, at shoulder level. For number *one*, the little finger is raised; for *two*, the next finger; for *three*, the middle finger is raised; for *four*, the index finger; and for *five*, the thumb, thus ending with all five fingers raised. For the numbers six through ten, keep the right hand as it is, with palm out and all five fingers extended. For *six*, touch your left thumb to the tip of your right thumb. For *seven*, raise the left index finger; for *eight*, add the middle finger; for *nine*, add the left ring finger; and for *ten*, the left little finger, so that all ten fingers are now raised.

Certain tribes indicate the numbers above ten by first making the sign for *ten*, then holding the left hand spread open with palm towards the chest, and then, with the right index finger, touching one by one the fingers of the left hand. The thumb stands for numbers *one* through *ten*; the index finger, *eleven* through *twenty*; the middle finger, *twenty-one* through *thirty*; the ring finger, *thirty-one* through *forty*; and the little finger, *forty-one* through *fifty*.

The right hand, in the same way, represents the numbers *fifty* through *one hundred*.

To indicate numbers over one hundred, raise both hands to shoulder level, thumbs touching, palms turned towards the person addressed, and describe an arc on the left side.

Hundreds are counted on the back of the left hand in the same way as for multiples of *ten*. It is sufficient to indicate at the outset that hundreds are to be counted.

Equal Place both hands in front of the chest, closed except for the index fingers, which are extended parallel to one another. Then move the hands towards the person being addressed, maintaining the same distance between the extended fingers.

Half Hold the left hand at chest level, palm facing right. Place the edge of the other hand on top of it and pointing towards the person addressed. The fingers are held together and extended. Then move the right hand to the right.

How much Make the sign for *much*. "How much money?" means "How many dollars?"

six

seven

eight

nine

ten

Much Raise the left hand, with palm towards the chest and fingers extended upward. Tap the left little finger with the right index finger, then tap the other fingers of the left hand. When the fingers are touched, they close up.

equal

half

Number Make the sign for *to count*.

Numerous Raise both hands fairly high on each side of the body and hold them vertically. The fingers are slightly crooked, forming a cup. Move the hands downwards, and then bring them close together. Once the hands are joined, palm to palm, lift them to the lower part of the chest.

One thousand Make the signs for *hundred* and *ten*. See text under *to count*.

thirty

much

numerous

to hear

to call (1)

to call (2)

to see

to cry (tears)

pain

The Body and the Senses

Bald Make the sign for *scalp*. Touch the top of the head with the flat of the right hand. Then make the sign for *to exterminate*.

Beard If the person giving the message has a beard, it is sufficient for him simply to point to it. If he has no beard, he cups his right hand and places the back of the hand against his chin, with the wrist out and the fingers extending down, like the hair of a beard.

Blind Close your eyes and place your palms against them. Then make the signs for *to see* and *not*.

Blood Bring the right hand up to the level of the mouth, with the index and middle fingers touching the nostrils. Lower the hand with a jerky and agitated motion.

Bone Make the signs for *dead* and *long time*. Then touch the part of the body where the bone is located. Lastly, point to some white object.

Brain Touch the forehead with two fingers of the right hand.

to Call, to be called This is one of the most important and most widely used signs. Tightly close your right hand and hold it in front of your face, with the thumb touching the other fingers and the knuckles pointing towards the person addressed. Then point the index finger, at the same time moving the hand slightly forward. This sign can also mean "What are you asking?" or "What is your name?"

Cold Bend your body slightly forward, close your hands and hold them at chest level. Make

to taste, tongue

beard

your hands and forearms tremble, as if you have a chill.

to Cry, tears   Place both hands clenched against the cheeks, with the index fingers pointing towards the eyes. The index fingers then suggest tears, which leave streaks on the cheeks.

Face   Open out your right hand and pass it over your face from top to bottom.

Headache   Make the sign for *sick*. Shake the right hand at forehead level to indicate stabbing pain.

to Hear   Hold the right hand cupped close to the right ear. By wrist movements, turn the hand slightly backwards and then forward.

Heart   Place the right hand, fingers held together, on the chest at the level of the heart.

Hot   If it is a question of the weather—sunlight, for example—place the palms behind the head, a short distance away from it. Then bring both hands forward so that they are in front of the head.

Liver   Place the hands over the top right of the abdominal cavity, where the liver is, and make them tremble slightly.

to Look   Make the sign for *to see*.

Lungs   Hold the right hand on the chest, with fingers stretched and spread.

Pain   Place the right index finger parallel to the spot where it hurts. Then make the sign for *sick*.

face

Scalp, head of hair   To indicate the human head of hair, touching one's own skull is enough.

to See   Place the right hand near the right side of the nose, with the index and middle fingers extended, and the other fingers clenched.

Sick   Spread your hands and place them against your chest. Then rub yourself in several places to indicate pain.

to Smell   Bend the right hand, palm horizontal, fingers spread, and bring it up to the nostrils. Raise the hand a bit more so that the nose comes between the tips of the fingers.

to Taste   See *tongue*.

Tongue   Stick the tip of your tongue out slightly, and touch it with the tip of your index finger.

Tooth   Turn your face to the other person. Hold your mouth half open, and with the right index finger point to the middle upper teeth.

blood

cold

hot

11

Life in the Tribe

All, everyone With the right hand held horizontally, palm down, describe a circle, going from right to left. Bend your body while you are doing this.

Ancestors Most tribes use the sign meaning *old man* (walking with a stick).

Bless you Raise both hands, palms facing outwards. Then lower them slightly and direct them gently towards the person addressed.

Camp Make the sign for *tepee* by crossing the index fingers to suggest a tent. Then, holding the arms horizontally at chest level, outline an incomplete semi-circle on each side. Then raise the hands slowly a short distance, by a slight movement of the elbows.

Campfire Begin by pretending to assemble something. Then make the signs for *wood, fire, to sit down* and *to speak*.

Chief Raise the right hand, index finger pointing up, to the level of the face. Then raise the hand as high as possible and, making a clockwise circular motion, depict a succession of arches, each one lower than the previous one.

Church Make the signs for *God* and *house*.

City Make the signs for *house* and *much*.

Council, tribal (in a circle to talk) Hold the hands tightly closed in front of the chest, with the little fingers touching and the palms facing the chest. Then move the hand so as to describe a horizontal circle, bringing the hands together again when the circle is complete. Then make the sign for *to speak*, first on the right and then on the left.

Corral Make the sign for *tree*. Then put both hands together with the fingers interlaced, giving them the appearance of a rail fence. Then spread the hands and make a semi-circle with each hand so as to form a circle.

to Dance Place both hands at chest level, fingers pointing up, palms facing chest. Raise and lower both hands two or three times.

Doctor Consists of the signs for *Paleface, to see* and *medicine*.

seated

chief (1)

chief (2)

to sing

council, tribal (1)

council, tribal (2)

private conversation

handshake

to listen

man with a future

all, everyone

everyone has gone

corral

Everyone has gone Hold both hands at chest level, fingers touching the palm in the direction of the other person. Then slowly pass the right fingers over the palm of the left hand. Then move the left hand behind the right hand.

Evil, devilish Make the sign for *bad*.

God (or the mystery of the universe) Make the signs for *medicine* and *big*, then point the index finger towards the sky.

to Graze a horse Make the signs for *horse* and *grass*. Then bring the left hand in front of the chest, with the thumb raised conspicuously. Then close the right hand over the left for a moment.

Handshake Squeeze the hands together in front of the chest. Indians did not shake hands except on great occasions such as the signing of a treaty or agreement, or the end of a war or a battle. After the coming of the Palefaces, the gesture became customary.

Hello, good day Make the signs for *sunrise, day* and *good*.

to Hint Make the sign for *to speak*.

Hospital Make the signs for *houses, sick* and *much*. Some tribes simply make the signs for *house* and *medicine*.

to Joke Hold the right hand at mouth level, palm turned towards the face, fingers slightly spread and half closed, the tips pointing forward. Move the hand forward and up. This sign is very seldom used.

Junior (in the sense of inferior in rank) Hold both forearms parallel, with the tip of one index finger held a little lower than the other. Vary the space between the two hands according to the size of the gap in rank.

to Laugh Hold both hands cupped, palms up, fingers raised and separated from one another, at chest level. First raise the hands, then lower them.

to Listen Turn your right side towards the other person, holding your right hand half closed, with only the index finger extended. Then raise the hand to your face and touch your earlobe.

to Make bad medicine First make the sign for *bad*, then the sign for *medicine*.

Life in the Tribe

to Make good medicine Make the sign for *good* and then the sign for *medicine*.

a Man with a future Make the sign for *man*, then raise the left hand to neck level, palm facing outwards, thumb and index finger extended, the other fingers slightly bent. Do the same with the right hand, but hold it slightly lower than the left. After a moment or two, raise the right hand higher than the left.

Me, myself Extend the left thumb and touch it to the middle of the chest.

Medicine (in the sense of the mysterious or the unknown) Hold the right hand at forehead level, palm turned inwards, middle and index fingers spread out and pointing up, the other fingers closed. Raise the hand higher and make a clockwise circular movement.

Motion pictures Of course, this is a fairly recent sign. Some Indians are well acquainted with the cinema—Chief Dan George, who proved himself a remarkable actor in "Memoirs of a Paleface"; and Iron Eyes Cody, a leading specialist in sign language, an established actor and a first-rate technical consultant on Indians. The Indians have thought up a number of signs for the cinema. The most widely used consists of holding both hands wide open, side by side (no doubt to symbolize the screen). Shake the hands slightly (probably to simulate the flickering of the projector). Then make the sign for *to see*. Some Indians, who have been present during filming and who have appeared in films, make the sign for *owl* to indicate the cinema—the eyes of the bird representing the camera lenses. They follow this by pretending to turn a handle. (This sign must predate sound movies, since the use of cranks went out when sound came in.)

Name When an Indian asks someone his name, he makes in succession the signs for *question*, *you* and *call*. "How are you called" means "What is your name?"

to Pray Make the signs for *to work* and *medicine*. Certain tribes in the Southwest follow this by raising both hands, open, and placing them at either side of the head.

Priest Make the signs for *clothing* and *black*. The first missionaries to venture into the West

joke (1)

joke (2)

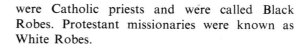
bless you

were Catholic priests and were called Black Robes. Protestant missionaries were known as White Robes.

Private conversation Hold the left hand on the left side of the chest. Then make the sign for *to speak*. Then move the right hand to a position under the left hand.

School Make in succession the signs for *house*, *white, to see* and *to know*.

Seated Close the right fist and bring it in front of the chest. Then lower it with a sharp movement to the level of the waist.

to Sing Hold the right hand in front of the mouth, with the index and middle fingers extended and spread out, the other fingers closed. Then describe a faint circle horizontally. To finish, make the sign for *all*.

Vaccination Make in succession the signs for *white, medicine* and *man*. Then point your right index finger and pretend to prick the left arm between the elbow and wrist.

medicine (1)

medicine (2)

work

Village Make the signs for *tepee* and *much*.

Wager (in the sense of gambling) Since it doubtless concerns a card game, the sign consists simply of pretending to put down chips or coins as a stake.

We, ourselves Make the signs for *me* and *everyone*.

We two, the two of us This refers to the two persons using sign language. First put the right index finger on the chest. Hold the other hand at face level and, moving the left arm to the side, spread the index and middle fingers to indicate the number two.

Whiskey Make the signs for *water* and *fire*.

Work Place the hands together in front of the chest, the fingertips of the left hand touching the palm of the right hand. The right hand should be held slightly higher than the left hand. Then raise both hands, shaking the wrists.

Yes Place the back of your right hand against the right side of your chest near the shoulder. The index finger should be extended and pointing; the other fingers should be closed, with the thumb resting on the middle finger. Move the hand slightly to the left and at the same time crook the index finger in the direction of the thumb.

The Bison Dance (by George Catlin)

Every summer the different nomadic Indian bands making up a tribe gathered and set up their tepees in a circle. The gathering marked the beginning of the big bison hunt. The hunt was preceded by ritual dances, which the Indians believed would promote the arrival of bison herds. The dances lasted until the herd was sighted, which might not be for three weeks. If one of the dancers became tired and stopped dancing, his companions would pretend to kill him and to dismember him, as though he were a beast.

The Indian Nations

Apache (Seeker of Moose Antlers) Make the sign for *Indian*. Then rub the right index finger against the left index finger, starting at the base and moving to the tip, then going back to the base. Repeat this several times.

Arapaho (Mother of All the Tribes) First make the sign for *Indian*. Then close the right hand and tap it two or three times against the left side of the chest, which means *mother*.

Blackfoot Make the signs for *moccasin* and *black*.

Black race Make the signs for *Paleface* and *black*.

Cherokee (Indians of the Forest) Make the sign for *tree*. Then hold your right fingers together and slowly raise them, spreading them out as you do so. Finally, rub the left palm with the tip of the right hand to specify that it is an Indian.

Cheyenne (Finger Cutter) Make the sign for *Indian*. Then extend the left index finger, place the extended right index finger on top of and perpendicular to it, and move the right index finger back and forth against the left one in a sawing action. This is also a sign for *mourning*.

Chippewa (Indians of the Woods) Make the signs for *tree* and *people*.

Comanche (Snake Indians) Make the signs for *Indian* and *snake*.

Crow Make the sign for *bird* and then the sign for *Indian*. Some tribes make the sign for *Indian* and then hold the right hand closed against the forehead, fingers facing the person addressed and held slightly higher than the top of the head to suggest the hair style used by Crow men.

Dakota Make the sign for *Sioux*.

Half-breed or mixed blood Hold the right hand on the middle of the chest, slightly curved, fingers together and pointing up. The fingers should turn towards the right, with the little finger nearest the body. Move the hand 10 inches (25 cm) to the left, then bring it back to its original position. After a very slight pause move the hand about 10 inches (25 cm) to the right. Some Plains tribes

Two warriors – an Osage and an Iroquois – with a Pawnee woman. The Plains Indians were divided into tribes, which in turn were made up of bands or clans, each with a chief and his followers. Men chose a bride from outside the clan. This custom was beneficial to the health and strength of the race, since it avoided the dangers of excessive intermarriage.

Paleface (white race)

make the signs for *half* and *Indian*, then the signs for *half* and *white*.

Indian Extend the left hand, palm down, and rub the back of it with the right fingertips, from the wrist to the fingertips. Do this at least twice.

Navaho (Tribe Whose Men Make Striped Blankets) Make the signs for *to work*, *blankets* and *striped*.

Nez Perce (Tribe Who Pierce Their Noses) Hold the right index finger under the right side of the nose. Then push the index finger to the left, passing it under the nose.

Osage (Indian Word Meaning Shaven Head) Make hand gestures that suggest cutting hair. Move the fingers as though they are scissors and glide the hands along the head from top to bottom.

Paleface, white race Hold the right hand horizontally, palm down, in front of the forehead at the level of the eyebrows. Then move it to the right.

Pawnee (The Wolf Tribe) Make the sign for *Indian*. Then place the right hand near the right shoulder, middle and index fingers pointing upward and palm facing the person addressed. Then raise the right hand.

People Hold both hands side by side at chest level, the backs of the hands facing the chest. Stretch the index fingers upward and bring the tips of the thumbs together, keeping the other fingers closed. Then move each hand farther towards its own side. Some tribes place both hands on the chest, backs of the hands facing outwards.

Shoshone (Eaters of Sheep) Make the signs for *Indians*, *sheep* and *to eat*.

Sioux (Throat Cutter) Hold the right hand horizontally, palm down, just below the chin and move it quickly to the right. This is the sign for the *Dakota* nation.

Ute Make the signs for *Indian* and *black*.

Indian

Cheyenne

Crow

Nez Perce

Osage

Pawnee

Sioux

future

Time

after

afternoon

sunrise

before

day (1)

day (2)

After Execute the sign for *time*, then pass the right hand over the back of the left hand.

Afternoon Make an incomplete circle with the right thumb and index finger. Then raise your hand behind your head and bring it down in the direction of the horizon.

Age First indicate the number of years, then make the sign for *winter*.

Always Place the right hand, open, at ear level. Move it slowly forward, then back. Repeat this. Then pass the hand in front of the head, and then behind it.

Before Hold both hands in front, index fingers pointing towards the person addressed. Follow this with the sign for *time*. Then thrust out the right hand and then pull it back.

Day Hold both hands horizontally at chest level about 4 inches (10 cm) apart, palms down. Then move them to each side, turn palms up and stop.

Dawn Hold both hands open and horizontally,

palms turned towards the chest, the right hand positioned above the left, the right little finger touching the left index finger. Then raise the right hand slightly to simulate the rising sun.

Eternity Open your right hand and place the palm against your cheek. Then move the hand from left to right twice. Finally, pass the hand in front of and then behind the head.

Fast Hold the hands in front of the chest, the right somewhat forward of the left and with the fingers together and extended straight ahead. Then pass the right hand rapidly over the left hand. Then touch the left palm with the right fingertips.

Forever Place the left hand against the left side of the face over the ear, and bend it forward and then backwards twice. Then pass the left hand in front of and behind the head.

Future Make the sign for *time*. Then bring the right hand forward, with index finger still extended, and pass it over the left hand.

Last year Make the signs for *winter* and *beyond*.

now

noon

night

often

time

fast

forever

Long time Make the sign for *time*. If it concerns the *past*, hold the arms in front, with both index fingers pointing forward, the right index finger held slightly behind the left. Then move the right hand towards the waist. If the *future* is involved, the movements are reversed. Both hands are near the waist, the right index finger positioned slightly behind the left. Stretch the right arm forward.

Midnight Make the signs for *night* and *middle*.

Morning Make the signs for *day* and *sunrise*.

Much time Hold the left arm horizontally, fist closed. Then touch the left wrist with the extended right index finger. Then move the index finger in several arching hops up the left arm towards the elbow. The sign is also used to say *often*, *all the time* and *instant*.

Next year You must indicate the season. In winter, one thinks of the summer to come, so make the signs for *winter*, *to finish* and *grass*. In summer, one thinks of winter, so the signs to make are those for *autumn*, *to finish* and *winter*.

Night Extend both hands, held open, about a foot (30 cm) apart. The palms should be down and

the right hand should be slightly higher than the left. Then cross the wrists, placing the right wrist over the left.

Noon Make the signs for *today* and *middle* to show that the sun is at its zenith.

Now Hold the right index finger, extended upwards, about 8 inches (20 cm) in front of the face. Move it a few inches forward, stop, and almost immediately move it forward again.

Often Hold the right forearm horizontally in front of the chest and extend the left forearm forward. Touch the left forearm several times with the right index finger, beginning at the wrist and moving towards the shoulder.

Past Make the sign for *before*.

Rapidly Make the signs for *work* and *fast*.

Right away Make the sign for *future*. Then pass the right hand in front of and behind the head. Some tribes make the sign for *to wait*.

Setting sun Make a semi-circle with the right thumb and index finger. Then bring the right hand down to the side, to symbolize the setting of the heavenly body. Done in reverse, this sign means the *rising of the moon*.

Sunrise With the right thumb and index finger, form an incomplete circle, keeping the other fingers together. Extend the right arm horizontally, pointing left. Then raise the hand about a foot (30 cm).

Time The Indians have different ways of indicating time. A common way is this: Hold both hands at chest level, index fingers pointing forward, the other fingers closed. Then pull the right hand back and to the right about 8 inches (20 cm).

Today Make the sign for *now* and then the sign for *day*.

Tomorrow Make the signs for *night* and *day*. Then, with the left hand, indicate the sun rising in the east.

Twilight, sundown Make an incomplete circle with the right thumb and index finger, keeping the other fingers together. Point the right arm horizontally towards the right, then raise the hand about a foot (30 cm).

Where?

The Bison Hunt (by George Catlin)
The Indian was usually mounted on a horse specially trained for this dangerous activity. The horse galloped alongside the bison and pulled away in a rapid bolt when the bison, wounded by a fatal arrow, lashed out blindly with all the fury of a beast in desperate straits. These horses had a notch in one ear to distinguish them from the other horses. Sometimes violent collisions made accidents inevitable: horse and rider, knocked down, perished under the hoofs of the maddened herd.

When Make the sign for *question* or *how much*. Then, depending on the duration of time involved, make the signs for *to sleep, moon* or *winter*.

Year Make the signs for *winter* and *now*.

Yesterday Make the sign for *night*. Then bring both hands forward, with the fingers partially closed. The left hand should be moved a little to the right and rotated a little so that the palm is turned upward and the hand forms a cup.

Aboard Hold the left hand, open and with palm up, a short distance from the body. Close the right hand and place it, with the little finger down, on the left hand.

Above The two hands are held flat, the right (with palm down) on top of the left (with palm up). Then raise the right hand slowly, keeping the left hand motionless.

Across Hold the left hand horizontally, about a foot (30 cm) from the chest, with palm down and extended fingers pointing towards the right. Then place the right hand over the left hand and slide it, fingers forward, over the top and towards the ground.

Among Hold the left hand, with fingers spread and pointing upward, about a foot (30 cm) from the chest. Then point the right index finger downwards and pass it between each of the left fingers in a snakelike pattern.

Below Place the left hand upon the right hand, with palms down, at chest level. Then lower the right hand vertically, the distance varying with the depth you wish to indicate.

Beside Make the sign for *near*.

Beyond Extend the right hand in front of the chest, fingers slightly apart. Move the left hand, fingers pointing down, over the right hand. Then shake the left hand, making it describe a slight arc upon the right hand, while turning the left palm gradually up.

Far The right hand is held on the side at shoulder level. Then move it forward slowly. If the distance involved is great, move it forward as far as possible.

Here First make the sign for *to sit down* and then move the right hand away from the face. Some tribes use only the middle finger.

middle

In the middle Make a horizontal circle by joining both thumbs and both index fingers, halfway up the chest. Keeping the left hand in its position, remove the right hand, place it above the left and point the right index finger downwards at the middle of the circle described at first.

Middle Hold the left hand in front of the chest, index finger extended downward, the other fingers closed. Then, holding the right hand beneath the left, make a semi-circle with the right thumb and index finger directly below the pointing left index finger.

Near Open your left hand and hold it vertically in front of you. Bring the right hand up to it, with the extended right index finger lying lengthwise on the left palm.

to Question Hold the right hand open, fingers spread, palm turned towards the person addressed, at shoulder level. By wrist action turn the right hand slightly, two or three times. If the person addressed is standing at a distance, raise the hand much higher and wave it from right to left. This means *what?* and occasionally *where? why?* and *when?*

up

Up Point to the sky with the index finger.

Where Make the sign for *question*. Then point the right index finger in several directions.

aboard

beside, near

across (1)

across (2)

beyond

above (1)

above (2)

below (1)

below (2)

among

calm down

affection

friend, friendship

sorrow

anger

fright (1)

fright (2)

Affection   Make two fists and cross the arms against the chest.

Afraid, cowardly   First point to the person in question. Then make the sign for *fright*.

Afraid of no one   Point the right index finger in several directions. Then make the signs for *to fear* and *not*.

Anger   Place the right hand, closed, against the forehead, with the thumb touching the forehead. Slowly bring the hand forward, rotating the fist slightly clockwise and counterclockwise in a twisting motion.

to Argue violently   Make the sign for *quarrel*.

Astonishment   Place the left palm or fingers on the mouth and extend the right hand, palm turned outwards, towards the person addressed, holding it about a foot (30 cm) from the chest. This sign conveys strong surprise, great satisfaction or deep disappointment.

Calm down   Hold the hands open at shoulder level, palms turned towards the person addressed. Then lower the hands slowly with a downward movement of the forearms.

to Desire, to want   Hold the right hand closed very near the chin. Then form an incomplete circle with the thumb and index finger at mouth level. With a slight wrist movement, bring the hand to the lips, thus making the motion of drinking. The little finger should be at the same level as the index finger.

Disgust   Make the signs for *heart* and *tired*. This feeling is sometimes expressed by a simple facial expression.

to Disturb   Make the sign for *heart*. Then place the right hand on the heart. Finish by making the sign for *perhaps*, while shaking the hands.

Emotions

astonishment

madness

rashness, irresponsibility

jealousy

pity (for others)

pity (for oneself)

shame (1)

shame (2)

Drunk Make the sign for *whiskey*, then the sign for *to drink*. Repeat this four or five times. Then make the signs for *much* and *mad*.

to Endure Gently place the open right hand on the left side of the chest. Then raise the right hand and hold it to the right of the face, the palm facing inwards and the fingers held together.

Enemy The signs for *friend* and *not* are most often used. Some tribes make the signs for *to shake hands* and *not*.

Extravagant Cross the wrists a short distance from the heart, with the right wrist closest to the chest and with both hands closed. Press the right forearm against the body and keep the left wrist on the right wrist. This sign is also used to indicate *madness, tenderness, affection, thoughtlessness* and *love*.

Fear, to fear Make the sign for *fright*.

to Forget Make the sign for *night*, followed by a vigorous forward movement of the right

hand. Then sweep the right hand towards the left side, passing over the left hand.

to Forgive Raise both hands, closed except for extended thumbs and index fingers, to shoulder level, with palms facing the person addressed. Then move the hands forward, each describing a semi-circle. Then make the sign for *to go*.

Friend, friendship (or *brother* and *people who live together*) Raise the right hand to neck level, palm out, index and middle fingers touching and extended. Then lift the hand until the fingertips reach the level of the face.

Fright Hold both hands, palms down, at chest level. The right index finger is extended and the other right fingers are closed, while the left hand is completely closed and held slightly closer to the chest than the right. Then half-close the right hand.

Gloom, melancholy, sadness Make the signs for *heart* and *sick*.

Feelings

to Groan, to moan With the hands held horizontally, make the motion of cutting the hair just over each ear (to suggest scalping). Then make the signs for *to call* and *hard*.

Happy, contented Make the signs for *heart* and *day*.

to Insult If it refers to another person, make the signs for *to work* and *bad*. If it refers to yourself, make the signs for *to do*, *me* and *bad*.

Intense, severe (cold, pain, etc.) Make the sign for *mad*.

Jealousy Close both hands and place them against each side of the chest. Then move the right elbow both to the right and towards the rear. Then do the same with the left elbow. Repeat at least once.

Joyous Make the signs for *heart* and *content*.

to Love Make the sign for *friend*.

Mad, madness Close the right hand and place the knuckles of the fingers against the forehead. Then rub the hand against the forehead in a counterclockwise circular pattern. (This direction means the *sun*; the opposite movement means *medicine*.)

Pity, compassion Raise both hands, palms facing inwards, in front of the chest, with arms extended and only the index fingers pointing upward. Then bring both hands towards the chest.

Quiet Thrust both hands forward at chest level, with palms down and fingers together. Then lower the hands very slowly to the level of the waist.

Rashness, irresponsibility Place the left hand over the eyes and raise the right hand to neck level, with the right index finger pointing forward.

Sad Close the right hand and place it against the forehead. Then with the same hand, execute a small circular movement, keeping it in the same place, however. The head should be turned to one side and the face should have a serious expression. If the head is kept straight, the sign means *mad*.

to Scold, to reproach Make the signs for *to speak* and *bad*.

Shame With the fingers held together and extended upwards, the rear edges of the hands are placed against the cheeks. Then the hands are crossed diagonally across the face.

Shy Make the sign for *shame*.

Sorrow Make the signs for *to cry* and *tears*. Then pretend that you are cutting your hair.

Surprise Make the sign for *astonishment*.

Timid Make the signs for *not* and *brave*.

to Trouble, to worry Make the sign for *heart*. Then wave your hand in the direction of the heart.

shy

The Bear Dance (by George Catlin)
During the bear dance, the hunters imitate the movements and attitudes of the grizzly, an animal that symbolizes strength and courage. Most of the dancers only wear a mask; however, the medicine man, who directs the ceremony, is dressed in a complete bearskin. With this dance, the Indians hoped to obtain the good will of this dangerous animal, which would then let itself be killed, when the time came, without endangering the lives of the hunters.

Wi Jun Jon (Pigeon Egghead), son of an Assiniboin chief, was invited to Washington in 1832 to represent his tribe, and to have the honor of shaking hands with the Great White Father (the President). As he went down the Missouri on a boat, he began notching his pipe stem to record the white man's houses that he saw. When there was no room left on the pipe, he continued the count on a stick, and then on another stick. There still wasn't room enough. At St. Louis he gave up and threw all his sticks overboard. In Washington, Wi Jun Jon attended receptions, shook hands with the President and drew smiles of admiration from the ladies. He was taken on a tour of the East, to show him the power of the Paleface. Ever alert, he visited several large cities and seaports and all that he saw was inscribed in his memory. He went back to his tribe rigged out in a colonel's uniform, with a plumed hat, gilded epaulets, an umbrella and a fan. His people barely recognized him. On top of this, he told stories about the Palefaces that were totally unbelievable. The Assiniboins quickly came to regard him as the biggest of all liars. Later he was blamed for practices that appeared to indicate that he possessed a dangerous power. His people decided to put him to death. Thus was the sad fate of a man shot in the head for having told nothing but the truth. (By George Catlin)

Qualities and Faults

bitter

sharp

lame

brave, courageous (1)

brave, courageous (2)

short

emaciated

distant

hard, strong

thick

fatigue (1)

fatigue (2)

Alert Make the sign for *to see*; then point the right index finger in several directions, shifting the hand rapidly. Then do the signs for *much*, *to sleep* and *not*.

Ambitious Make the sign for *people* and *push*.

Bad Hold the right hand clenched at the level of the left side of the chest. Then lower it towards the left side, opening the fingers one by one.

Big Make the signs for *sizeable* and *high*.

Bitter Touch the tongue with the tip of the right index finger and then make the sign for *bad*.

Brave, courageous Place the left hand, clenched into a fist, at a distance of about 8 inches (20 cm) from the middle of the chest. Then make a fist with the right hand and hold it just above and slightly to the right of the left hand. Lower the right hand by dropping the right forearm so as to graze the left hand in passing. Some tribes use the signs for *heart* and *strong*.

Contemptible Make the signs for *heart* and *small*.

Crippled Make the sign for *lame*.

Dangerous If a person is meant, make the signs for *heart* and *bad*. If a place is meant, make the signs that explain why it is dangerous.

Dark (in the sense of gloomy or overcast) Make the sign for *cloud* and then pass your hands behind your head.

Deaf Put the right palm against the right ear. Then make a slight circular movement with the same hand, held slightly away from the ear. Finish by making the sign for *not*.

Deep To indicate the depth of a river or stream, begin by making the signs for *watercourse* or *water*. Then point the right index finger towards the ground to indicate depth. If it is very deep, outline a person or horse to give an approximate notion of the river's depth in comparison to the height of the man or animal.

Distant Hold the right arm to the side at shoulder level. Move it forward slowly. If the distance is considerable, extend the arm as far as possible.

Divine Point the index finger towards the sky and look upwards with a respectful attitude.

large

high

honest

sizeable, big

Emaciated, gaunt Make the sign for *poor* in the sense of poor in quality.

Fast, rapid Raise the left hand to chest level and move it towards the left side of the body. Do the same with the right hand, keeping the hands about 6 inches (15 cm) apart. Then quickly pass the right hand in front of the left, describing a slight upwards curve first, then a downwards one.

Fatigue Hold both hands at waist level with the index fingers pointing forward. Lower the hands in a weary manner with the index fingers pointing at the ground, and the other fingers still clenched.

Frankness In succession, make the signs for *truth, day* and *good*.

Generous Make the signs for *big* and *heart*.

Good Place the hand horizontally at the level of the heart, with the fingers extended towards the left side of the body. Then shift the hand, still in a horizontal position, towards the right side of the body.

Hard See *strong*.

Heavy Hold both hands stretched out in front of you, palms turned up. Do this gesture as though you were encountering resistance.

High With fingers together and palms turned towards the ground, hold the right hand a short distance from the right shoulder, then raise it to the desired height.

Honest Make the sign for *true*.

Indiscreet Begin with the sign for *mad*, continue with *rashness* and finish with *small*.

Inferior, lower (in the sense of position and rank) Close the hands, index fingers pointing up. One index finger, representing the subject, is placed slightly lower than the other. If several persons are referred to, the right index finger is placed much higher than the fingers of the left hand.

Innocent Raise both hands, held open, to shoulder level, palms turned towards the other person. This means "I have nothing in my hands, I am unarmed."

Judicious, wise Make the sign for *heart*, then point the right index finger forward and conclude by making the sign for *good*.

inferior, lower

Lame Keep the right hand closed, palm down, about a foot (30 cm) away from the right side of

wide (1)

wide (2)

heavy

thin

27

the chest. Move the hand slightly forward and by wrist action lower the hand a bit towards the left.

Liar, to lie (in other words, to have two tongues) Hold the right hand at the right side of the mouth, with fingers aimed to the left. Move the hand forward in such a way that the fingers pass in front of the mouth.

Light, clear Hold the hands open, with fingers spread out, palm up, at an equal distance from the waist. Raise the hands briskly while shaking the wrists.

Little (in the sense of not much) Raise the half-closed hands to shoulder level, with the tips of the fingers crooked and facing the fingers of the other hand. The palm of the right hand should be at the level of the left index finger, about 10 inches (25 cm) away. Then raise the right hand above the left, then the left above the right. Then raise the right above the left again.

Live Make the sign for *living*.

Living Place the right hand about a foot (30 cm) away from the chest, index finger extended; then by wrist action make three zigzags.

Long Hold the two index fingers parallel. Push the left one forward, then draw the right one back to a point just behind the left.

Narrow Make the sign for *little* in the sense of not much.

New Make the signs for *old*, *not* and *good*.

Old See *old man*.

Open Hold both hands open horizontally, palms up. The hands should be in contact with one another and the fingers thrust forward. Spread out the fingers, with the two little fingers touching.

Paralyzed Hold both hands against the chest, palms turned towards the ground, and make them tremble slightly.

Poor (in quality) Half close your hands and bring them together as if you were rearranging something in front of you. Then separate them slightly, placing the right index finger on the base of the left thumb.

Poor (opposite of rich) Hold the right hand closed at chest level, thumb near the body. Lower

bad (1)

bad (2)

paralyzed

poor

sick

deaf

and Faults

vile, horrible

small

dark, gloomy, overcast

old

living

thief

the arm quickly, moving it forward at the same time, keeping the hand closed, and by a wrist movement make the thumb face forward.

Proud Make the signs for *painted, clothing* and *to find*. Or, place the right hand opened out against the mouth and throw the head back. Finish by making the sign for *good*. This expression in sign language literally means *good clothing*.

Remote Make the sign for *distant*.

Rich Make the signs for *possession, much* and *pony* or *horse*.

Sharp Hold the left hand open, palm up. Gently rub the side of the little finger with the tip of the right thumb. Then make the sign for *good*.

Short Hold the left hand on the left side of the chest, fingers together and pointing upwards at the height you wish to indicate.

Sick Spread out the hands and press against the chest; then rub yourself in several places to express pain.

Sizeable (big) Hold the hands with the palms facing each other, fingers spread, at chest level. Keep the hands fairly close together at first, then spread them out, the right hand stretching to the right and the left hand stretching to the left.

Small Hold the left arm at shoulder level, palm up, the other fingers clenched in such a way that the tip of the index finger is below the thumbnail.

Smooth Make the sign for *prairie, rock,* or *cliff,* depending on the circumstances. Then make the sign for *wash*.

Soft Make the signs for *hard* and *not*.

Sour Extend both index fingers, keeping the other fingers clenched and touch the tip of the tongue with them. Then make the sign for *bad*.

Strong Some tribes make the sign for *brave*. Others first raise the right hand above the left hand and tap the front and back of the left hand, bending the fingers as if breaking a thin stick.

Sweet Make the sign for *sugar*.

Thick Touch the palm of the left hand, held at chest level, with the right thumb, firmly grasping both the palm and back of the left hand. Repeat this four times.

Thief Make the signs for *people* and *to strip*.

Thin If possible, outline with your finger something slender or pointed. Hold the left hand open, palm up. Using the right thumb, held above the other fingers of the right hand, rub the fleshy part of the left palm and also use the right little finger to rub the back of the left hand at the same time. Make this sign very carefully, for it bears a strong resemblance to the signs for *thick* and *bacon,* which are the exact opposite. If you make the sign for *bacon,* follow it with the sign for *to eat*.

Tiny If it involves an animal, outline the size; if a quantity, make the sign for *little* in the sense of not much.

Ugly Hold the right hand against the face, the fingers touching the forehead. Then describe a faint circle on the front of the face. Finish with the sign for *bad*.

Uncertain Make the sign for *maybe*.

Undecided Make the sign for *maybe*.

Vile, horrible With fingers of the right hand spread, press the right thumb on the right cheek.

Vulgar Place the back of the right hand on the left hand. Then make the sign for *bad*.

Weak Make the signs for *strong* and *not*.

Wide Make the sign for *big*.

Wild Make the sign for *alone*.

The Family

Aunt According to circumstance, make the signs for *father* and *sister*, or *mother* and *sister*.

Baby Place the right hand clenched against the left side of the chest, palm inwards. Clasp the right forearm with the left hand as if holding a baby.

Bachelor Make in succession the signs for *man*, *marry* and *not*.

Blood brother Make the sign for *Paleface* or *Indian*, as the case may be and then slowly raise the right hand to indicate the height of the person, the index finger being pointed upwards.

Boy Make the sign for *son*.

Brother Touch the tips of the index and middle fingers to the lips. Then make the sign for *man*.

Brother-in-law Fold the arms across the chest, the left arm below the right, hands open flat. Then lower the right arm, keeping the elbow against the body until the right forearm is horizontal.

Child Make the sign for *man* or *girl*, as the case may be. Hold the right hand closed against the right side. Then indicate the size of the child.

Divorce Make in succession the signs for *woman* and *to abandon*.

Father Cup your right hand slightly, and tap the right side of your chest gently two or three times. Then make the sign for *man*.

Father-in-law According to circumstance, make the sign for *woman* or *husband* first. Then make the sign for *father*.

Girl, daughter Place your hands on the sides of your head, with fingers bent. Then lower your hand as though using a comb. This sign can also be done with the right hand only.

Grandmother Make the signs for *mother* and *age*; then bring the right hand near to the right ear and describe a circle to indicate that she is hard of hearing.

Husband Make the signs for *man* and *to marry*.

Little girl Make the sign for *daughter*, then with the right hand closed, indicate the height of the child.

Male Make the sign for *man*.

baby

son

woman, wife

brother

boy

girl, daughter

to marry

mother

father

Daily Life

Man Stretch out the right index finger, keeping the other fingers closed, palm facing the other person. The same sign means *male*.

Marry Make the sign for *exchange*, then hold both index fingers together pointing forward.

Mother With the right hand half closed, give two or three gentle taps on the left side of the chest.

to Name Make the signs for *to call* and *to give*.

Old man Clench the right hand and pretend to be leaning on a cane or stick, while bending forward. Then make the sign for *man*.

Sister Make the sign for *woman*, then hold your index and middle fingers horizontally with their tips on your lips, with the thumb and other fingers closed up.

to sleep

Son Make the sign for *man*, then with the right hand closed, index finger extended upwards, indicate the child's height.

Woman, wife Make the signs for *girl* and *husband*.

Bed Hold the left hand, palm up, at chest level. Bring the other hand, palm up also, slowly towards and under the left. Then make the motions of spreading a blanket, and finish with the sign for *to sleep*.

Birth The left hand is held a short distance from the chest, palm up. With the right hand, make the motion of pulling something energetically towards you.

to Boil Make the signs for *water* or *food*, then those for *kettle* and *fire*.

to Break camp or move Make the sign for *tepee;* then with the hands still in the same position, pretend to take down the poles. Then make the signs for *to work, to wrap* and *departure*.

Coal Make in succession the signs for *hard, fire* and *good*.

to Cook Make the signs for *to make* or *to work;* then for *to eat* or *good*.

to Drink Turn your side to the other person. Cup your right hand and draw it slowly up to your lips as if you were drinking. This same sign is also used for *water*.

to Eat Cup your right hand to resemble an upside-down bowl or basin. Keeping the hand on a horizontal plane, move it towards the mouth. Then pull it away and move it back towards the mouth, repeating this several times. This sign can also mean *to get provisions*.

Famished, hungry Make the sign for *to cut* and *half*. Hold the right little finger against the middle of the chest, then wave it to the right, then to the left.

House, home With the hands open and placed against the chest horizontally, interlock both sets of fingers at right angles to one another.

Satisfied Close the right hand, extend the right index finger. Bring the hand to stomach level and

to drink

to eat

satisfied

bed

Daily Life

then raise it as high as the chin and hold it there briefly.

Sit down, stay   Hold the right hand clenched into a firm fist at shoulder level. Then lower it briskly 4 inches (10 cm).

to Sleep   Hold both hands open with palms facing each other, and place them on the right side of your head. Then tilt your head to the right and pretend to sleep.

Smoke   Hold the clenched left hand in front of the middle of the chest, with your right hand about 4 inches (10 cm) beneath it. Lower the left hand until it touches the right hand. Repeat this two or three times. Then make the sign for *pipe*.

Tepee   Place both hands in front of the chest, quite close together, with the index fingers touching and forming a 60° angle. Some tribes make the same sign but keep the last joints of both index fingers in contact, to symbolize the poles that stick out at the top of the tepee.

Tent   Face the other person, holding your hands at chest level. Spread your hands slightly, keeping the tips of both index fingers touching one another, forming an inverted V.

to Wash   Make the sign for *water*, then pretend to wash something.

SOME SIGNS FOR FOOD

Bacon   Hold your left hand in front of your chest with the palm up. Rub the thumb and index finger of your right hand against the little finger of your left hand, back and forth. Repeat this two or three times. Then make the sign for *to eat*.

Bread   Make the sign for *flour*, then slap your hands together as though you were kneading dough. The right should be above the left, and both held horizontally.

Cherry   Make the sign for *tree*, then pretend to pluck fruit with the left hand. Make motions as though collecting the fruit in the right hand. Then close the right hand and pretend to squeeze the juice into the left hand which is held cupped.

Meat   Hold the right hand open, palm down, over the left hand, also open but palm up. Then with the fingers of the right hand, rub the inside of the left hand.

Milk   Hold both hands closed, a short distance apart, and then alternately raise and lower each hand, as though milking a cow.

Salt   Touch the tip of the tongue with the end of the right index finger. Then pull the hand away from the face and rub the thumb against the index finger, as though sprinkling something on a dish.

Salted   Point to the ground with the right index finger. Then lower the arm, hold it crooked against you, and rub the thumb against the tips of the other fingers.

Sugar   Touch the tip of the tongue with the tip of the outstretched index finger, keeping the other fingers clenched. Then make the sign for *good*.

Tea   Make the signs for *tree, leaf, to drink* and *good*.

bacon

meat

The Arrow Game
The Indians were inveterate gamesters. They would bet all their possessions and even their scalps and their lives. Here is depicted the arrow game which consisted of shooting a maximum number of arrows in a minimum time, so that the greatest number would be in the air before the first one fell to the ground. (By George Catlin)

Action Signs

to advance

to bring (1)

to bring (2)

to break (1)

to break (2)

to hide

to Accompany   Hold the left hand on the left side, fingers together and pointing forward. The elbow should be against the body and the fingers should be on the same plane as the forearm.

to Add   Place the right hand on top of the left, palms touching. Slowly raise both hands, without separating them, to a height of about 4 inches (10 cm). Repeat this gesture several times.

to Advance   Hold both hands out at chest level, both with palms down and fingers pointing towards the person being addressed. The left hand should extend slightly farther out than the right. Move both hands forward at the same time in brief jerky movements.

to Arrange   Make the signs for *work* and *to fasten*.

to Begin   Place both fists against the waist, arms held tight against the sides. Move the hands forward, pretending to make an effort. This sign may be used to mean *to push*.

to Break   Close both hands, hold them fairly close together and raise them. Then spread them, with the right hand tipping to the right, the left to the left, to suggest breaking.

to Bring   Move the right hand away from the body, with index finger extended, then draw the hand back, bending the index finger in.

to Burn   Make the sign for *fire*, then show what burned or was destroyed by fire. If the object has been completely consumed by fire, make the sign for *exterminated*.

to Catch   Make the sign for *to take*.

to Choose   This is a very simple and much used sign. Simply point the right index finger in the direction of the person or thing referred to.

to Climb, go up   Hold the right hand at elbow level, palm pointing up. Crook the forearm and raise the index finger almost to brow level.

to Close   Hold the right hand slightly closed, with the fingers placed in front of the right shoulder. Then holding the body erect and rigid, bring the hand down towards the torso.

to Crush   First make the sign for *pumpkin*. Then place both hands together, palms facing. Follow this by making strenuous motions as though kneading and flattening.

to Cut   The left hand is held horizontally at shoulder level, with the palm down. Do the same with the right hand, but keep it closer to the body, with the palm up. Pass the right hand under the

33

left hand, as if you were using a knife to cut something. Repeat this several times.

to Dig   Hold both hands side by side, with the fingers together and simulate the act of tapping the ground with a hoe. Repeat this several times making a curving motion.

to Dive   Hold the left hand vertically a short distance from the chest, fingers pointing towards the right. Hold the right hand behind the left, fingers together and pointing down. Then pass the right hand over the left.

to Do, to make   Make the sign for *to work*.

to Enter, entry   Make the sign for *house*, then place the left hand, closed, in front of the chest. Then pass the right hand, half closed, over and under the left hand.

to Extend   Make the signs for *to arrive here*.

to Extinguish   First make the sign for *fire*, then with palm up, extend the right hand over the point where you made the sign for *fire*. Lower the hand. Finish by making the sign for *to exterminate*.

to Find   Make the signs for *I, to see* and *to take*.

to Finish   Hold the left hand open in front of the body, parallel to the waist. Point the right hand forward and touch it to the right hand at a right angle. When the wrist comes in touch with the left hand, abruptly withdraw it.

to Give   Raise the opened right hand towards the side. Then point it forward and then upwards to shoulder height. Then move it outwards and down.

to Grasp   Bring both hands half open to a position in front of the chest. Close them briskly, and move them forward as though wanting to grasp something.

Grip, hug   Spread your fingers and crook them towards the ground, like the claw of an eagle. Make a fairly lively forward motion, as though to seize an object abruptly. Then bring the hand back very rapidly towards the body.

to Hang   See *to hook*.

to Hide   Place the left hand at a slight angle above the right hand. Then lift the right towards the left and pass it under the left.

to Hold   Turn the palms of both hands, with the fingers joined together, towards the chest. Then interlace the tips of the right fingers with those of the left hand, so that nothing can get through. Then separate the hands, keeping them in the position they were in, and move the right hand to the right and the left to the left, moving the shoulders and elbows at the same time.

to Hook   Thrust the left index finger forward, keeping the other left fingers clenched, at chest level to suggest a sort of hook. Then curve the

to cut

race

to sew

to give

to fasten

to keep

right index finger slightly, move it towards the left index finger and hook it onto the index finger.

to Hunt   Make the sign for *wolf*. Then bring both hands near the eyes and spread them out towards each side.

to Keep   Firmly grasp the left index finger with the right hand. Then move the hands slightly from right to left.

to Keep steady   Make the signs for *good* and *strong*.

to walk

to climb, go up (1)

to climb, go up (2)

to hang

to mix

to Keep still   Make the sign for *halt* two or three times; then raise the right gently as though to say "Don't be afraid."

to Lead astray   Make the sign for *to hide*.

to Mingle   Hold the hands half open, palms facing, fingers pointed up. The hands should be fairly close to one another. Then set them in a circular motion, maintaining the same distance between them.

to Mix   If you wish to describe the blending of several things, make the motion of stirring things together. If you wish to convey the notion of *to mingle*, make the sign for that word.

to Paddle   Make the sign for *boat*, and then pretend that you are paddling a canoe.

to Pull   Hold the hands closed, one against the other, at shoulder level, about 4 inches (10 cm) from the chest. Thrust the right hand slightly forward, drawing the left hand back an equal distance. Return to the original position and repeat.

to Push   Place both fists against the sides of the body, then move them forward, giving the impression of making an effort.

Race   First indicate the type of competition (for example a boat race). Then thrust both index fingers forward, making the sign for *equal*. For a horse race make the signs for *horse* and *race*.

to Receive   Make the sign for *possession*.

to Run after   Hold the left hand open at chest level, palm turned inwards. Do the same with the right hand, but hold it nearer to the body. Then rapidly move the right hand behind the left hand.

to Search   Make the sign for *wolf*.

to Sew   Hold the left hand closed, index finger extended, at chest level, with the palm facing the chest. Hold the right index finger behind the right thumb as though it were a needle. Move the right hand slightly to the right and the left hand to the left.

to Strip   Hold the right hand up, palm down, fingers clenched except for the index finger, which should be pointing outwards from the middle of the chest. Place the left hand a little above it,

to swim

the same with the left hand. When the left hand nears the bottom of the oval, bring the right hand up behind it and start over again. If animals are involved make the sign with both hands together.

to Write Hold the left hand open, with the back of the hand facing the other person. Then make the motions of holding a pencil between the right thumb and index finger and pretend to write on the palm of the left hand.

to dive

to push

to take

fingers together. Tap the left hand on the top of the right hand. At the same time, crook the right index finger.

to Surround Hold both hands about 4 inches (10 cm) apart, thumbs and index fingers extended, the other fingers closed. Bring both hands together so that the tips of the index fingers touch each other and the tips of the thumbs touch each other, thus forming a circle.

to Suspend Make the sign for *to hook*.

to Swim First make the sign for water. Then bring the tips of the fingers of both hands in front of the waist. Spread both hands to the side, imitating the breaststroke.

to Take Thrust the right hand rapidly forward, with the fingers closed except for the index finger which is pointing. Then close the hand in the direction of the body, making the gesture of bringing something to you.

to Walk, a walk If persons are involved, hold the hands open, side by side, against the front of the chest, fingers together, palms down. Move the right hand forward describing an oval. Now do

to separate

to come

to hold

The grizzly hunt is particularly dangerous. With one blow of his heavy steel-clawed paw, the fearsome bear can disembowel a man or a horse. The Indians often hunted him on horseback, but they wound up fighting him hand to hand, armed only with a knife. When made into a necklace, the claws of the grizzly were a sign of great heroism on the part of the wearer. (By George Catlin)

To keep his seat during the mad ride amid the thundering hoofbeats of the herd, the rider generally had his knees held by a belt girdling the pony. In addition, a long rope trailed from behind the pony, to be used to recover the mount in the event of a spill. Usually the hunter held both his bow and arrows in one hand, and let the arrows fly with amazing dexterity. (By George Catlin)

tree

canyon, gorge, ravine

to grow

grass

Apple   First make the sign for *tree*. Then with the thumb and index finger of the right hand, indicate the size of the fruit. Then point to something red and make the sign for *to eat*.

Autumn   Make the signs for *tree* and *leaf*. After this, pass the left hand below the waist in an undulating movement.

Bay   First make the sign for *water*. Then with the right hand at chest level, sketch the shape of an inlet.

Bean   Hold the right hand horizontally, palm up, fingers together.

Brook   Make the signs for *watercourse* and *small*.

Brush, thicket   Raise the hands to symbolize grass; then extend the hands out from the waist.

Canyon, gorge, ravine   Raise the closed hands together, almost in front of the face and fairly close to it. Then, keeping the left hand in place, use your right hand to make a gesture suggesting entering a canyon.

Cliff   Make the sign for *mountain*. Then lower the fist to give an idea of the height and size.

Cloud   Hold both hands as high as possible above the head, with the index fingers touching. Then lower them gradually and shake them as you do so, to symbolize a descent from the sky.

Corn (maize)   Hold the left hand horizontally, thumb and index finger extended, to symbolize an ear of maize. Then rub these two fingers with the right thumb and index finger.

Country (geographical area)   Extend the right index finger towards the earth. Then stretch both hands towards the right and left.

Country (homeland)   Place both hands flat on the ground. Then raise them slightly, stretching them towards either side.

Dam   Make the signs for *watercourse* and *to hold*.

Drought   Make the signs for *long time, rain* and *not*.

Earth (also used to mean territory)   Extend the hands horizontally and raise them to chest level about 7 inches (15 cm) apart. Then slowly lower them together to mid-thigh height.

Evening   Extend the right hand and make the sign for *sunset*. Then make the signs for *night* and *small*.

Extent   The place referred to is shown in relation to the sun. The right thumb and index finger are directed towards the left side, to indicate that the sun rises in the east. Therefore the right side stands for the west and the north is behind the person making the signs and the south in front of him.

Fall (of leaves)   Make the sign for *autumn*.

Fire   Place the right hand in front of the body, fingers nearly closed. Then raise the hand gradually, spreading the fingers. Do this over two or three times.

Flower   Make the sign for *grass* at waist level. Make a wide circle out of the thumbs and index fingers of both hands. Hold the hands so that the little fingers are touching.

Fog   Make the sign for *water*. Then cross the hands below the eyes with fingers spread.

Footprint   Make the signs for *to walk* and *to see*, then point to the ground with the right index finger.

Forest   Hold both hands 8 inches (20 cm) from the shoulders, with the backs out, thumbs and

lightning

water

fire

leaf

forest (1)

forest (2)

fingers extended. Slowly raise them a bit to indicate growth. Extend the right hand towards the right, then bring back to the front, to indicate a wide expanse.

to Freeze   Make the signs for *cold*, *water* and *hard*.

Fruit   Make the sign for *tree*. Then, with the right thumb and index finger, make a circle to indicate the size of the fruit. Raise the hand as though plucking fruit from branches. Finish with the sign for *to eat*.

Grain   Hold the right hand at chest level, palm up, fingers closed, with the thumb against the index finger, to symbolize a vessel holding grain.

Grass   Hold both hands palms up, fingers raised, fairly close to the ground. Then raise the arms, shaking the hands slightly as you raise them.

to Grow   Hold the right hand close to the ground, on the side, fingers closed, except for the index finger which is pointing up. Then raise the hand, index finger still pointing up, in a succession of jerks.

Hail   Make the signs for *rain* and *cold*, then indicate the size of the hailstones by making a circle with the right thumb and index finger.

Hill   Make the signs for *small* and *mountain*.

Hole   Make a circle with the thumbs and index fingers of both hands. Then raise the left hand, while the right hand remains on the chest.

Ice   Make the signs for *water* and *cold*. Then join your hands together.

Ice blocking a stream   Make the signs for *cold* and *water*, then open both hands and turn the palms down, fingers extended, at shoulder level. Move the hands towards each other until the index fingers touch. This sign stands for the ice that forms on the surface of water.

Icicle   Make the signs for *ice* and *water*, then point to the ground with the right index finger, hand held at shoulder level.

Island   At chest level make an incomplete circle with the thumbs and index fingers, but not touching one another. Hold the left hand in position and with the right hand make the sign for *water*. Then close the right hand and with the fingertips trace a second circle surrounding the first.

Lake   Make the sign for *water*, then with the thumbs and index fingers of both hands, trace an incomplete circle about 8 inches (20 cm) in diameter. Finish by shaking the wrists, with the fingertips spread.

Leaf   Make the sign for *tree*. Then raise the right hand in front of the right shoulder. The index finger and thumb, slightly bent, are pointing forward and upwards. The other fingers are closed. Raise the open left hand, fingers spread, palm facing you. Make the hand tremble slightly, to simulate the trembling of leaves.

Light   Make the sign for *day*.

Lightning   Hold the right index finger, pointing up, near the bottom of the left cheek, at jaw level. Then move the hand away, describing several zigzags in the air from left to right.

Metal   There actually is no sign for this. Sometimes the sign for *hard* is made, and then a metal object is pointed out.

Meteor   Make the sign for *star*, then with the right hand make the sign for *fire*. Then drop the right hand abruptly with a snaky movement.

Midwinter   Make the signs for *winter* and *middle*.

Nature

Migration Make the signs for *bird, much* and *to fly* in a north-and-south direction.

Moon (referring to both the satellite and the months) Extend the thumb and index finger of the left hand, with the other fingers closed, palm facing the person addressed, who sees something resembling a crescent. Then make the sign for *night* and finish by pointing to the place where the moon is supposed to be.

Mountain Hold the right hand as you would for the sign for *cliff,* but much higher. Then make the sign for *effort.* Use both hands if it refers to a mountainous region.

Mud Grasp the fingers of your left hand with your right hand at chest level. Lower the hands together, after which reverse the positions of the hands. The fingers of the right hand are now held by the left hand. Lower the hands together. This gesture suggests an animal floundering in mud. Depending on the situation, next make the sign for *effort* or those for *not* and *effort.*

Near a spring First put the tips of the right index and middle fingers to the lips, as in the sign for *brother.* Then make the sign for *near* or *far,* according to the distance of the source of water.

Pass (in the mountains) Extend the right thumb and index finger and raise the right hand from the right side towards the middle of the chest.

Peak Join the right fingers in a sort of cone. Then raise the hand from waist level to face level.

to Plant Make the signs for *maize* and *to work.* Lean forward and with the right hand, starting at the right shoulder, make the gesture of putting something in the soil.

Potato Hold the fist closed against the ground, leaning forward as you do so. Raise the hand without opening it, with the back of the hand up. The potato was a staple crop for many tribes.

Prairie Hold both hands open in front of the chest, side by side, fingers together, palms up. Then separate them, the right hand going to the right and the left to the left.

Pumpkin (a very popular vegetable in some tribes) First bring your hands together to form a sort of ball, with the fingers spread and half open. Then with the right index finger, point to something yellow.

Rain Hold both hands closed very high above the head, about 8 inches (20 cm) apart. Lower them slowly, opening them as you do so, until the fingers are all opened out when you reach the level of the waist. Repeat this slowly two or three times.

Rainbow Make the signs for *rain* and *to finish.* Then, with the right hand extended, palm down, describe a semi-circle in front of you to symbolize the rainbow.

Rapids Make the signs for *watercourse* and *rock.* Then hold the right hand near the chest, fingers spread and pointing forward, and lower it with a shuddering motion.

Region First point to the ground nearby with the right index finger. Then extend both arms to the right and left.

Rock Make the sign for *hard* and give an idea of the size.

Rose Slowly raise the left hand, half closed, fingers together. Then with the right hand, also half closed, pull on the tips of the left fingers, as though plucking petals.

Season Use the signs for the individual seasons.

maize

metal

mountain

island

lake

moon

winter

hill

snow

cloud

peak

to shine, to sparkle

sun

Shelter   Hold both hands about 4 inches (10 cm) apart in front of the middle of the chest. The fingers are closed except for the two index fingers, the tips of which are touching each other. Then open the other fingers, including the thumbs, which, until now, were apart from one another.

to Shine, to sparkle   First make the sign for *star*. Then raise the index finger above the other fingers. Finish with the signs for *short* and *private conversation*.

Snow   Hold both hands almost closed fairly high in front of you, palms turned towards the person addressed. Slowly lower them in a pattern of zigzags and curves to symbolize glitters and swirls.

Spring (season)   Make the signs for *grass* and *small*.

Spring, well   Make the sign for *water*. Then hold both hands close together, thumbs and index fingers touching to form a little circle. Then with the right hand half closed to form a sort of cup, pretend to drink.

Star   Make the sign for *night*. Then make an incomplete circle with the right thumb and index finger and wave the right hand towards the sky. For a twinkling star do all this and then place the right hand on the outstretched left arm, just above the hand.

to Submerge   First make the sign for *water*, then the sign for *lake*. Finish by making the sign for *to die*.

Summer   Make the sign for *grass*, raising the hands very high. Some tribes make the signs for *sun* and *hot* above the head.

Sun   Make an incomplete circle with the index finger and thumb of the left hand. Then extend the hand towards the east and describe a curve moving west.

Thunder   Make the signs for *bird* and *fire*. Then raise the right hand slightly in front of the head and above it. (The Indians believed that thunder was produced by the Thunderbird.)

Thunderbolt   Point the right index finger forward at a certain height, then drop the hand abruptly to indicate a thunderbolt striking the ground.

Tornado   Make the signs for *wind* and *attack*.

Tree   Place the left hand 4 inches (10 cm) from the shoulder, palm towards the chest, thumb and fingers spread. Shake the hand very slightly to symbolize growth.

Water   Cup the right hand just in front of the mouth, fingers aimed to the left and raised up. Then make the sign for *lake* or *watercourse*.

41

Nature

Watercourse Extend the right arm, hand out, index finger pointing, the other fingers closed. Then bring the hand back as far as the shoulder.

Waterfall First make the sign for *watercourse*. Then raise the left hand, palm turned towards the chest, fingers together. After this, pass the right hand over the left, right fingers extended and spread. Then move your hand as though starting to go over the edge.

Wind Hold both hands horizontally in front of the chest, palms down, fingers together and pointing forward. Move both hands forward, shaking them to symbolize the blowing of the wind.

Winter Hold both fists in front of the chest, with the backs of the hands facing the person addressed. Shake the hands to symbolize the fall of snowflakes.

Wood Make the signs for *tree* and *to cut*.

World Hold both hands horizontally in front of you, fingers together, thumbs touching, at waist level. Then move the hands away from one another.

spring (well)

earth

hole

wind

The Bison Hunt
In this picture, the painter George Catlin depicts himself downwind of a herd of bison, accompanied by two guides. In the first half of the 19th century, the great herds of wild ruminants had not yet been wiped out as they were later by such Palefaces as Buffalo Bill and his kind. The prairie sheltered an abundant and varied fauna, in spite of its harsh climate and immense treeless expanses.

George Catlin, painter of the Indians, was born on July 26, 1796, at Wilkes-Barre, Pennsylvania. He devoted his whole life and his incredible energy to the defense of his Indian friends, tirelessly struggling to make them known and loved. At the time when the Plains Indians were at the height of their power, Catlin visited 48 tribes in 8 years and painted 310 portraits and 200 other oil paintings. He organized numerous exhibitions in the United States, England (where he was received by Queen Victoria), and Europe. In France he exhibited at the Salle Valentino on June 3, 1845, then at the Louvre, where he was received by King Louis-Philippe. Unfortunately, Catlin was not understood. He died a ruined man, consumed by tuberculosis, on December 23, 1872, in Jersey City, New Jersey.

Following his death, his works were finally collected in 1879, after much difficulty, by the Smithsonian Institution in Washington. The magnificent original hand-tinted lithographs reproduced in this book came from a famous work now impossible to find: "Catlin's North American Indian Portfolio," London, 1844—25 lithos (4 cm x 62.5 cm). Collection of Daniel Dubois.

Jos-o-sot (Walking Bear), chief of the Sacs of the upper Missouri, painted by George Catlin. The chief, either hereditary or elected, served more as a counselor than a commander. His personal valor more than anything else defined his authority. When he lost the confidence of his people, he was replaced. A certain number of notables (40 among the Cheyenne) shared responsibility for the problems of war and peace.

(By George Catlin)

Bison Hunt in Winter (by George Catlin)
During the long winter months, when the prairie was covered with snow, the Indians put on snowshoes and hunted bisons, both for meat and for the warm hide. The animals had difficulty escaping, sinking up to their bellies in the snow, and thus were easy marks. The hunters killed them with arrows and spears.

Mortally wounded, the old male utters long cries as he goes through the final agonies. Blood streaming from his gaping wounds stains the snow dark red. The hunters, panting, knives in hand, get ready to dismember the carcass, which will go towards keeping their clan alive.

Animals

bison

beaver

moose

deer

horse

Bear The Crows and those tribes close to them simply put the hands on either side of the face at ear level, with the fingers curved and the fingertips slightly forward to imitate the animal's ears. Other tribes wanting to be more precise, moved the hands down from the forehead in imitation of a bear about to use his fearsome claws.

Beaver Hold the left hand a short distance from the chest, palm down. Then do the same with the right hand, holding it slightly lower. Raise the right hand, then lower it to suggest a beaver slapping its tail on the ground.

Bird Place the hands horizontally at shoulder level, palms down. Imitate the beating of wings. If it concerns small birds, wave the hands briskly. For large birds wave them more gently.

Bison Hold both hands closed, with only the index finger pointing, and thumbs touching the joints of the middle fingers. Bring the hands to both sides of the head at the level of the temples, and raise them slightly until the wrists are above the head. Then gently move them forward.

Bison calf Hold both hands closed, thumbs pointed up, on each side of the face, to stand for the newly appearing horns of the young animal.

Cat (can also mean *flat nose*) With the tips of the right thumb and index finger together, touch the nose. Then move the right hand away slowly from the face, keeping the fingers in the same position. Then indicate the size of the animal.

Chicken Make in succession the signs for *bird* and *red*. Then place the right hand over the head to symbolize the comb.

Cow Hold the left hand closed, thumb pointing down. Grasp the thumb with the right hand and pretend you are milking a cow. Repeat this several times.

Coyote Make the signs for *wolf* and *little*.

Crow Make the sign for *bird,* by extending the hands forward, palms down, elbows touching the body. Then point to something black, while cawing like a crow.

Deer (stag) Symbolize the animal's antlers by holding the hands on either side of the head with the fingers spread.

Dog Hold the right hand forward, with the index and middle fingers extended. Then move it back.

Duck Make the signs for *bird* and *water*. Then with the right palm make a gesture outlining a small hill.

Eagle Extend the arms and wave the hands in imitation of the beating of wings, with the palms down and fingers stretched out. Then bring the right hand near the nose, curving it slightly to suggest the bird's beak.

Egg Hold the right hand at the level of the left breast, then make a circle by bringing the thumb and index finger together. Then make the sign for *bird*.

Fish Begin with the sign for *water,* then hold the right hand vertically on the side, fingers joined and thrust forward, at waist level. Move the hand forward with a snakelike motion to imitate the path of a fish in the water.

to Fly Make the signs for *bird*.

Fox Indicate the height and bulk of the animal. Indicate that the tail is *long* and *white*-tipped.

Frog Make the sign for *water*. Then slightly close the right hand and hold it at shoulder level. Make the movement of a frog jumping.

Goat This is composed of two parts. First place both hands at temple level, index fingers pointing up to suggest horns. Then bring the right hand below the chin to suggest a beard.

Goose Make the sign for *bird*. Then outline a triangle in front of you to indicate the triangular flying formation of migrating geese.

cat

goat

frog

wolf

owl

Horse Raise the right palm obliquely in front of the left side of the chest. To make the sign more forceful, some tribes put the left index and middle fingers astride the right hand.

Monkey (to the Indians, an animal half white man and half dog) Move the thumb and index fingers of both hands (other fingers are kept closed) in front of the chest and towards the lower part of the body. Then make the sign for *Paleface*. Pass both hands, as before, in front of the chest and finish with the sign for *dog*.

Moose Put the tips of both thumbs at a level with the ears. Then spread the fingers upwards. Finish by touching the front teeth with the index fingers.

Mouse Hold the left hand near the ground, half closed. With the same hand make the sign for *to walk* and *fast*. Finish with the sign for *night* and with the right thumb and index finger pretend you are nibbling the left index finger.

45

Animals

Mule Hold your hands above your head, palms facing the person addressed, fingers pointing up to represent long ears. Pivot the hands from the wrists to indicate the position of the ears.

Owl Make the sign for *bird*. Raise the right hand, slightly closed, on the right at shoulder level. Then move it quickly forward and down. Describe circles to suggest the owl circling in on its prey. Finish by placing the hands in front of the eyes, to suggest huge round eyes.

Pig Form a circle with the tips of the thumb and index finger of each hand touching those of the other. To symbolize the animal's snout, place the circle in front of the face at the level of the nose.

Pony Make the sign for *horse*. Indicate the size of the animal with the right hand open and extended.

bird

Prairie dog Hold the right hand on the right side. Lower it to indicate the size of the animal. Then make the sign for *hole*. Then tap the right hand against the closed left hand. Then close the index finger and thumb, make the signs for *small* and *to speak,* the latter to suggest the animal's characteristic cry.

Pronghorn Place both hands, open, palms facing the person addressed, on each side of the head, at forehead level.

Puma Make the signs for *cat, long, tail* and *to jump*.

Rabbit Use your right hand to give the size of the animal, then make the sign for *to jump.*

Rattlesnake Make the sign for *snake,* then extend the right index finger forward from the left shoulder. Then raise the right hand, keeping the index finger pointed. Wiggle the finger in imitation of the snake's tail.

Sheep (bighorn) Place the right hand half closed against the left temple and make a backwards circular motion to simulate the large horns of the animal.

Sheep (domestic) Place the right hand against the left temple and describe a backwards curve to symbolize the large horns of the sheep. Then make the signs for *mountain, jump* and *together*.

Skunk Hold your nose with the right thumb and index finger, to symbolize the animal's snout. Raise the fingers up to suggest the tail. Then make the sign for *bad.*

Snake Hold the right hand at waist level, the index finger pointing forward, the other fingers closed. Move the hand forward with a wavy motion to simulate the undulating movement of a snake.

Spider Hold the right hand horizontal, palm up, fingers spread and curved. Wiggle the fingers nervously to symbolize the spider moving over its web. The left hand remains motionless.

Squirrel Fully face the person addressed. Then hold your cheeks on each side of the mouth and move the lips quickly. This sign conveys the image of the animal eating a nut. Squirrels are very numerous in the forests of the United States.

Tail Put your hand behind your back (kidney level) and point to the ground with the index finger, keeping the other fingers closed.

Turkey Make the sign for *bird*. Then place the right hand, closed, under the chin, fingers pointing down. Wiggle the hand slightly using a wrist movement.

Wolf Hold the right hand at shoulder level, index and middle fingers pointed and spread, other fingers together. Then move the hand on a slant in front of you.

sheep

mule

bear

fish

During their great seasonal migrations, the immense herds of bison were followed by grey wolves, coyotes and other animals of prey, ever ready to attack an old male abandoned by the herd. Then a death struggle began but before the bison was overcome by force of numbers, many an assailant died on the yellowed grass of the prairie. (By George Catlin)

The Indian horse descended from Andalusian stallions introduced into Mexico by Cortez. What they lost in beauty in the severe winters of the American climate, they gained in stamina. The Sioux first called them Sunka Wakan (mysterious dog), then Ta Sunka (horse). By 1750, they roamed the prairie in numerous wild bands. They became the catalysts of a profound change that gave rise to one of the most picturesque cultures in human history: that of the bison-hunting Plains Indians. (By George Catlin)

The male bison was a magnificent animal 6 feet (11.8 m) tall at the withers and weighing up to 3,300 lbs (1,500 kg). At full speed they could go 29 miles (48 km) an hour and they lived to 30 years of age—provided they were not killed by Indians before then. The smaller female gives birth to a single calf at a time. Until the last century, the bison was the symbol of life to the Indian, for it provided for so many of his needs. Its near disappearance in the second half of the last century was equivalent to genocide. (By George Catlin)

Objects

Arrow Bring the left hand close to the chest, with the index finger and thumb forming a ring (as though holding a bow). Grasp the ring with the right hand and make the motion of pulling back a bowstring.

Automobile First make the sign for *wagon,* then pretend you are holding the wheel of a car. To represent an automobile the Cheyenne make the signs for *wagon, by itself* and *to go.*

Awl The right index finger simulates an awl or leather punch. Let it slide against the left index finger, held perpendicular, with the fingers forward. The left hand is supposed to represent the cloth or piece of leather to be stitched.

Axe Raise the right hand above the left arm, fingers together and extended, then lower it abruptly, as though splitting wood or slicing something.

Bag Simulate the opening of a bag with the left hand, then thrust the right hand through the

awl

match

bowl, cup

boat

candle

cartridge

kettle, cauldron

rope

imaginary opening, with the fingers held together. To indicate a large bag, use the arm to form an opening.

Bicycle Make the sign for *wagon,* but with the fingers close to one another. Then make the signs for *man, aboard* and *to go.*

Bit (for a horse) Place the right thumb and index finger on the sides of the mouth, with the rest of the hand resting on the chin. This sign can also mean *bridle.*

Blanket Close both hands and draw them up to the shoulders, as though pulling a blanket up on you. Then move the right hand towards the left and the left towards the right so that the arms cross and the right hand is closer to the body. Stop when the two wrists come into contact.

Boat Bring your hands together in a cup to represent the hull of a ship. Then move them forward to indicate travel. If a canoe is meant, make the gesture of paddling. If a rowboat, pretend to row. If a steamboat, make the sign for *fire.*

Book Hold both hands open, one against the other, at waist level and pretend to read. Some Indian tribes begin with both hands together and then open them as though opening a book.

Bow With the left hand at waist level, pretend to hold something, a bow in this case, while making the motions of pulling on the bowstring with the right hand.

Bowl, cup With the hands joined, make the shape of a cup.

Buffalo hide Make the signs for *bison* and *blanket*.

Bullet Touch the last joint of the left index finger with the right thumb. Then lower the right hand and quickly point the index finger. The last movement symbolizes shooting, while what precedes it represents loading the gun.

Calumet (ceremonial pipe) Hold the left hand at the level of the left shoulder, index finger pointing towards the mouth. Place the right index finger so that it forms an extension of the left index finger, with the right hand placed against the right cheek. The left thumb is kept raised.

Candle Raise the right hand to shoulder level, index finger pointing up. Then make the sign for *fire* with the left hand slightly directed towards the left. The right index finger is extended first and then slowly closed as it approaches the left hand.

Cannon Make the signs for *gun* and *big*.

Canoe Make the sign for *boat* with the right hand cupped at shoulder level. Then pretend to plunge a paddle in the water and push it.

Card Pretend to hold a group of cards in your left hand. Then with the right hand point to the location of the other players.

Cartridge Turn your right side to the person addressed, holding your right hand a short distance from the chest, thumb raised, index finger pointing. With the left hand pull the right thumb back slightly, as if loading a gun.

Cigar Make the sign for *tobacco*. Then hold both index fingers horizontally, side by side, and make them turn against each other.

knife (1)

knife (2)

blanket (1)

blanket (2)

Cigarette Make the signs for *cigar* and *smoke*.

Covered wagon Make the sign for *wheel*. Then raise both hands held open, palms up, fingers half open, to the level of the face. Then let both hands fall in a sweeping curve.

Drum First arrange both hands to simulate the shape of a drum. Keep the left hand in place and motionless and use the right hand as a drumstick. Pretend to strike the drum several times.

Flag Hold the right hand open at shoulder level, fingers together and pointing forward. Place the left fingers on the right wrist. Then shake the right fingers several times to suggest a flag waving.

Hatchet Make the signs for *axe* and *small*.

Kettle, cauldron Form an incomplete circle with both hands, the index fingers touching but not the thumbs. Drop the right hand and make the

covered wagon

Objects

flag

arrow

whip

axe

saddle

motion of lifting by passing it underneath. With the left hand pretend to grasp a handle.

Key   Squeeze the right thumb and index finger together and place them against the open palm of the left hand. Then make the motion of turning a key in a lock.

Knife   Hold the right hand open at the right side of the face at mouth level. Move it towards the left two or three times as if you were going to slice something held between the teeth.

Lasso (lariat)   Make the sign for *rope*. Then pretend to twirl and throw a rope at something. Finish by making the motion of pulling something with the right hand.

Match   With the left hand, pretend to strike a match on the right arm which is held on a slant.

Money   Hold the right hand halfway up the chest, with the thumb and index finger forming an incomplete circle. This is the same as the sign for *medal*. The Indians were very fond of medals and the whites bestowed medals abundantly on them in order to gain their confidence and favor.

Needle   Make the sign for *to sew*.

Newspaper   Hold both hands together horizontally, palms up and spread out. Then make the sign for *to see*.

Phonograph   With both hands draw a loudspeaker in the air. Then with the right hand imitate a record revolving. Then make the signs for *to listen* and *good*.

Pincers   With the right thumb and index finger, form pincers. Then bring them close to the hair or eyebrows, pretending to pluck hair, a common practice among the Indians.

Pipe   Hold both hands at mouth level, with the backs of the hands down. The left hand should be 4 inches (10 cm) from the chest. The right hand should be about 6 inches (15 cm) from the left. Then pretend to be smoking a calumet. Slowly move both hands forward and down in front of you. Then bring them back to their initial position. Now pretend to puff on a pipe, held between the thumb and index finger.

Powder   Hold your left hand at your left side, horizontally, palm up. With the tips of the right fingers make the motions of picking up something scattered on the palm of the left hand.

Railway   Make the signs for *wagon* and *fire*. Raise the right hand fairly high in front of the face. Finish off with the sign for *fast*.

Rattle   Raise the right arm, with the hand closed as if grasping the handle of some object, to the level of the right ear. Shake the hand in a persistent manner. (The rattle is an instrument of great importance in Indian life.)

Revolver   Make the sign for *gun*. Then make the sign for *six* to indicate a six-shooter. Raise the right hand with fingers spread and raise the left hand with only the thumb extended, the other left fingers being closed.

Rope   Raise the hands as in the sign for *after*. Then raise each hand to the level of the corresponding shoulder, with the index fingers pointing forward and the other fingers closed. Move the arms forward and describe spirals with the wrists.

Saddle Hold both fists at chest level, wrists touching only, hands spread apart with the fingers closed and together.

Saw Make the motions of sawing.

Snowshoes First indicate the shape and size. Then make the signs for *to walk, snow* and *good*.

Soap With both hands at waist level, make the motions of washing the hands.

Spoon First make the sign for *bison*. Hold the right hand near the left hand, then raise it towards the mouth as if about to sip.

Steamboat Make the signs for *boat* and *fire*. After this raise the right hand a little above the head.

Tobacco Hold the left hand open, palm up, fingers together. Place the edge of the right hand on the left palm. With the fleshy part of the right hand, rub the left palm in a circular manner, as though picking up bits of tobacco.

Tomahawk The Indians most often indicated this by symbolizing a hatchet with the right forearm and right hand, lowering the forearm as though striking something with the edge of the hand.

War club First show the size of the stone. Then indicate the leather thong that holds the stone to the handle. Then make the gesture of brandishing the weapon and of striking out towards the ground in front of you.

Warship Make the signs for *boat, fire* and *big*.

Wheel Describe a complete circle in the air with both hands, palms up, equidistant from the chest. The index fingers should point forward, the other fingers are closed.

Whip Hold the right hand raised, fingers closed, as if squeezing something, at shoulder level. Then briskly lower the hand as if snapping a whip.

powder

revolver

bag

calumet, peace pipe

tomahawk

money

pipe

Dress and Adornment

clothing, costume

color

coat

medal

moccasins

gloves

mirror

hat

Belt With both hands, make the motions of putting a belt around your waist and buckling it.

Black Make the signs for *night* and *similar,* or extend the hands in front of the forehead and close the eyes. To indicate this color, the Indians very often point to something black such as their hair or eyebrows.

Blue Make the sign for *color,* then point to something blue, usually the sky when the weather is fair.

Brown Make the sign for *color* and then point to something brown.

Clothing, costume Place your hands flat against the upper part of the chest and move them down to just below the waist.

Coat Place both hands on the chest. Then lower them towards the ground.

Color Rub the fingertips of the right hand in a circular pattern on the back of the left hand. Usually after making this sign, you point to an object having this color: the sky for blue, grass for green, hair or eyebrows for black. (Do not confuse this sign with the very similar one for *Indian* which consists of rubbing the left finger over the entire inside surface of the right hand.)

Color (when spots are involved) Rub the backs of your hands together. This means that the color is scattered.

Dress Place both palms on the collarbones. Then slowly move them down to the waist, as if putting clothing on.

Earrings Point the index fingers down alongside the ears, with the other fingers closed. Move the index fingers slightly to imitate the swaying of pendant earrings.

Gloves Pass the extended thumb and index finger of the left hand over the top of the right hand to show that the hand is covered.

Green Make the sign for *color,* then point to something green—the grass, for example.

Grey Make the signs for *white, small, black* and *small* in that order. Or make the sign for *color* and point to something grey.

Hat Hold the right hand out in front and trace a horizontal line two or three times, with the thumb and fingers closed. Then raise the hand until the thumb is at eye level. Extend the index finger towards the left and the thumb towards the right and pass them over the forehead, fairly close to it.

Leggings Pass the hands over the front of the legs, thumbs and index fingers clearly visible to the person addressed, the other fingers grazing the sides of the legs and the calves.

Medal Make an incomplete circle with the thumb and index finger of the right hand, the other fingers being closed except for the little finger which is placed on the middle of the chest.

Mirror Hold the left hand open, fingers crooked, 8 inches (20 cm) from the face, exactly as though you were looking into a mirror.

Moccasins Bend over so that you can touch your lower legs. Then place your hands flat against the shins, palms in, with the thumbs and index fingers pointing down and the other fingers squeezing the sides of the legs.

Painted Rub your cheeks and forehead with the fingers of the right hand.

Ring Hold the left hand open with palm down, fingers extended and spread, at lower chest level. Then with the tip of the right index finger touch the first joint of the fourth finger of the left hand, the ring finger.

Scented, perfumed With a movement of the wrist, bring the right hand up to the nose and touch the tips of the fingers to the nose. Then make the sign for *good*.

Shawl Make the signs for *woman* and *blanket*.

Shoes Make the signs for *moccasin* and *white man*.

Spotted, speckled Hold the left arm out in front, slightly inclined towards the ground. With the right fingertips touch it several times, proceeding towards the elbow.

Striped Hold the left arm out in front, as you would for the sign for *spotted*. Open the right hand, with fingers together and extended, and trace a stripe several times on the left arm, beginning at the wrist and proceeding to the elbow. Repeat this several times.

Tattooed Press several times with the right fingertips on the spot where the tattoo is. If it is on the right arm, use the left fingertips.

War bonnet Hold both hands open over the head, covering the head from the forehead well back. Then move the right hand back, as far down the back of the head as possible.

War paint Rub the right cheek in a circular motion with the tips of the right fingers.

Watch With the left thumb and index finger, make an incomplete circle. Then raise the right hand and point the right index finger downwards

war bonnet

at the circle. Then make the signs for *to see, to know* and *sun*. Then point to the dial of the imaginary watch, and indicate the movement of the hands in relation to the position of the sun.

White Make the sign for *color* and then rub the tip of the right index finger on the last joint of the left thumb, near the nail. Then point the index finger at something white.

Yellow Make the sign for *color* and point to something yellow.

ring

tattooed

war paint

earrings

On the Trail

Ahead   Make the sign for *to push*.

All is well   Make the signs for *all* and *well*.

to Arrive here   Hold the right hand a foot (30 cm) from the body, on the right side. Then, with thumb and forefinger extended, briskly move it close to the left hand, which is held against the the heart.

to Arrive there   Hold the right hand near the chest, index finger pointing up. Then bring it forward and, with the right index finger, tap the palm on the left hand, which is held open about a foot (30 cm) from the chest, palm turned towards the body.

Astride, on horseback   Separate the right index and middle fingers and bring them down so that they straddle the extended fingers of the left hand, which is held open and perpendicular, with the tips of the fingers pointed towards the person addressed.

to Avoid   Hold the hands at shoulder level, index fingers pointing up, the other fingers closed. Pass one hand in front of the other, then move them away from each other.

Bridge   Hold the hands side by side in front of the chest, palms up, fingers pointing forward. Then make the signs for *water* and *across*.

Burden   Place both hands flat on the forehead as if they are supporting a load. Bend the body forward slightly to give the impression of strain in carrying weight.

to Camp   Cross your index fingers at neck level to suggest a tent.

to Cross   Make the sign for *across*.

Departure   Make the sign for *to go*.

to Dismount   Make the sign for *horse*. Then point the fingers towards the ground.

Distance   The right hand is held to the side at shoulder level. Move it forward slightly. If the distance is great, move it as far as possible.

to Drive a wagon hitched to a horse   Make the sign for *horse,* then bring the hand forward in a succession of curves, as in the sign for *to ride a horse*. Then make the sign for *to sit down* on the left palm.

to Drive, lead   Hold the right hand at neck level on the right side, with the back of the hand facing the right, fingers closed and thumb pointing backwards. Then move the hand forward in fits and starts.

Dry   If you are referring to a stream or spring, make the signs for *watercourse, water* and *all gone*.

Dust   Point the right index finger towards the ground. Then move it slightly forward and down. With the fingertips pretend that you are rubbing the ground (and thus stirring up a small cloud of dust).

to go ahead of

to arrive here

to drive, lead

to go

to trot

to dismount

to arrive there (1)

to arrive there (2)

to wait

to camp

to meet, to encounter

astride, on horseback

bridge

departure

together

To capture a wild horse, the Indian used the tactics of the prairie wolf, tracking the animal relentlessly. When the exhausted horse stopped at last, the young brave would approach it slowly with his lasso made from plaited bison hair. With a precise and rapid movement, he would throw the lasso. The animal, half strangled, would kick until tired out; then it would calm down. The red man would then breathe softly into its nostrils. Pacified, the mustang would leave with its new master. (By George Catlin)

On the Trail

Fall, to fall Hold the left hand horizontally open, palm down, at lower chest level. Hold the right hand in the same posture 8 inches (20 cm) above the left. Then strike the back of the left hand with the palm of the right. Another way: Hold the right hand at chest level, horizontally and open, palm down, and simply lower it abruptly.

to Float Begin with the sign for *water*. Then place the left hand, held open and horizontally, palm down, in front of the right side of the chest, and place the right hand over it. Then move both hands in an undulating manner towards the right side.

to Follow Hold your hands in front, palms facing each other. Move the left hand slightly forward and then thrust both hands forward in a zigzag movement.

Footprint Make the signs for *to run* and *equal*.

to Gallop Begin with the sign for *to ride a horse*. Then hold the hands open about a foot (30 cm) apart in front of the chest, palms facing each other and extended fingers pointing slightly upwards. The left hand is near the body, the right farther away. Move the hands upwards together, then lower them several times, describing curves, in imitation of a horse on the trail.

to Get down (from a wagon) Move both hands from the waist towards the ground.

to Get lost Make the sign for *track,* then point the finger in several directions, one after the other.

to Go Hold the right hand near the chest, palm up, fingers together and extended. Then move the hand briskly towards the person addressed.

to Go away Raise the right hand, palm turned towards the person addressed. Wave the hand forward and bring it down in a wide curve to the right side. Repeat this two or three times.

Group Make the sign for *patrol.*

to avoid

to float

fall

trap (1)

trap (2)

to fall

sledge

Halt Raise the right hand, palm out, fingers together, to a point a little above shoulder level. Then move the hand very slightly forward and stop it abruptly. Some tribes energetically raise the right hand very high.

to Hurry Make the signs for *work* and *rapid*.

to Jump Close the right hand slightly, with palm up, the fingers together and pointing forward at shoulder level. Then move the hand forward in curves that suggest jumps.

Last, final Hold the hands out in front of the chest, then bring the index fingers together. Then rapidly move the right hand down and back. This symbolizes the last horse in a race.

to Leave, go away Make the sign for *to go.*

to gallop

to Meet, to encounter Hold the arms out, wide apart, hands facing the ground, index fingers extended, the other fingers closed. By bending the elbows, bring the arms in front of the chest until the tips of the index fingers are touching.

Pitfall Make the sign for *trap*. Finish by bringing both palms together.

to Ride a horse First make the sign for *horse*. Then move the hands forward, making a succession of small curves.

Safety Hold the right hand open at shoulder level, fingers together, palm towards the person addressed. Describe a circle with the same hand, moving it clockwise.

Scout Make the sign for *wolf*.

Sledge Hold the hands 8 inches (20 cm) apart at chest level, palms up, with index fingers partially extended in crooked position, the other fingers closed. The tips of the folded middle fingers are covered by the thumbs. Move both hands forward slightly.

Slowly Hold your hands in front, palms facing each other, 8 inches (20 cm) apart. Move them slowly forward, making brief stops as you do so.

to Stop Using both hands, make a grasping gesture, with the fingers slowly closing, in front of the chest. When the fingers are fully closed, cross your wrists.

Together Make the sign for *near*.

Track Make the sign for *to walk* and then point to the ground.

to Transport Hold the right hand at shoulder level, closed except for extended thumb. Next, put the left thumb against the right hand. Next, go through the motions of carrying something, leaning forward a little as if bent beneath a load.

Trap If it is a steel trap, first touch a metal object. With hands at chest level, join the tips of your thumbs and index fingers to make a complete circle directed towards the person addressed.

Before horses were in wide use by the Plains Indians, hunters used tricks to hunt bisons. They knew that the bisons were used to the constant presence of wolves and paid little attention to them. They therefore dressed themselves in wolf pelts and crawled up on all fours, armed with bows and arrows. When they reached the right distance, they would quickly shoot one arrow after another into the herd, killing a large number of animals all at one time. (By George Catlin)

Next, curl the thumbs closed, point the index fingers at the ground and bring them together.

to Travel Make the signs for *track* and *to see*.

to Trot First make the sign for *horse*. Then bring both fists in front of the chest, with the right one slightly in front of the left, palms down. With the right hand imitate a horse's forelegs trotting, and with the left hand do the same for the hind legs.

to Wait Make the sign for *halt*. Then bring the left arm up, hold the left hand in the same position as the right, and slowly lower the arms from the elbows. Then stop them abruptly.

Walk If people are involved, hold the hands in front of the chest, side by side, palms down and fingers extended and held together. Then describe an oval in the air with your right hand. Do the same with the left hand. When the left hand is down, move the right hand over it and begin again. If animals are involved, do the gestures with the hands joined.

On the Warpath

friend

attack, assault

wounded, wound

capture (1)

capture (2)

to Aim (a weapon) If it involves a gun, make the gestures of shouldering and pointing a weapon towards the object to be shot. If a bow, pretend to hold one in your left hand, and with the right hand pretend to tug on a bowstring to draw back an arrow.

Alliance First make the sign for *peace*. If the alliance is made for the purpose of waging war, make in succession the signs for *to go, war* and *together*.

Artilleryman Make in succession the signs for *Paleface, soldier, together* and *cannon*.

Attack, assault Make the sign for *charge*.

Barracks Make in succession the signs for *Paleface, soldier* and *house*.

Battle Make the sign for *combat,* then the one for *to shoot,* with both hands pointed in the direction of the person addressed.

Bayonet (weapon used by white soldiers) First make the sign for *rifle*. Then join both hands vertically, the right higher than the left, with the index fingers pointing.

to Beat, to hit Hold the left hand open, palm up. With the flat of the right hand strike the palm of the left hand as though clapping. This gesture especially refers to blows given with a weapon.

to Capture Clutch your shoulders with your hands. Then, with closed fists, cross your wrists in front of your body.

Charge (in the sense of rushing forward) Hold both hands closed at the level of the right shoul-

der, fingers facing the person addressed. Then move them forward, progressively opening out your fingers.

to Destroy Make the sign for *to exterminate*.

to Die, death Hold the right hand vertically, palm turned towards the chest. Hold the left hand under the right, with the left index finger pointing towards the right hand. Move the left hand forward, passing it under the right hand, describing a slight curve.

to Encircle See *trap*.

Escape Close both hands and place one wrist on the other. Then separate them with an abrupt gesture, thrusting the left hand to the left side and the right hand to the right side. Then make the sign for *to go*.

to Escape from Place the right hand, with the index finger extended, in front of the chest. The forearm should be horizontal. Raise the hand so that the forearm becomes vertical. Make a pivoting movement with the hand. This symbolizes avoiding a danger or recovering from illness.

to Exterminate Place the inner edge of the left hand on the chest, with the palm up. Then tap the left hand with the right hand.

to Fight Hold your hands tightly clenched and slightly in front of you, at shoulder level. Then move them briskly towards the person addressed. Repeat this several times.

Fire (in the sense of combustion) Make the sign for *to shoot at*.

to Flog Make the sign for *to exterminate*.

combat

to shoot at, gunshot

to imprison

Fort Make successively the signs for *white, soldier* and *house.*

Friend Raise the right hand to shoulder level, with the index and middle fingers extended upwards and held together, and with the other fingers closed.

Gun Pretend to shoot, then make the sign for *fire*. If you wish to be more precise, add a gesture imitating the pulling of a lever.

Horseman Make the signs for *Paleface, soldier* and *ride a horse.*

to Imprison Raise the left fist and move it backwards and to the left, with the little finger pointing towards the chest at shoulder level. Then grasp the left wrist with the right hand. Lastly, cross both wrists, hands closed, in front of the chest, with the right wrist over the left.

Infantry Make the signs for *Paleface* and *to walk.*

to Kill Half-close the right hand and hold it in front of the right shoulder. Then thrust it towards the left and slightly downwards, diagonally across the chest.

to Patrol Make the signs for *wolf* and *to see.*

Peace Place the hands in front of the chest, with the left palm turned up.

Powder Hold the left hand in front, palm up. With the fingertips of the right hand, pretend that you are assembling something from parts scattered over the left palm.

Prisoner Cross your wrists, with the right wrist on top, as if they are tied together.

escape (1)

escape (2)

to seize

to Recruit Close both hands, palms up, and hold them in front of the chest, with the left hand held horizontally and the right hand resting on it. Then rub the hands against one another in a roundabout movement.

to Rescue, to release Make the signs for *to seize* and *to go.*

to Resist Make the sign for *to sit down.*

prisoner

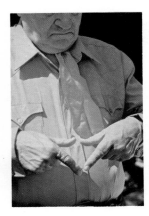

to encircle

soldier

to exterminate

Warpath

to kill

Retreat Make the sign for *charge,* to convey the idea of attack. Then, with a movement of the wrists, turn the hands so that the fingers are pointing backwards.

Reverse Make the signs for *heart* and *bad.*

Ruse, stratagem Make the sign for *wolf.*

to Seize Make the sign for *possession.*

Sergeant Make the signs for *Paleface* and *soldier.* Then, with the right index finger, trace a sergeant's stripe on the left forearm.

to Shoot at, gunshot Hold the left hand closed near the upper part of the chest, palm down and closed except for the thumb, which is extended laterally. Then move the hand down a short distance in a slanting motion, extending the fingers one by one.

Smoke signal For a far-off signal make the sign for *fire.* Then lift the right hand until it is over the head.

Soldier Hold both hands closed at chest level, palms down and thumbs touching each other. Then separate the hands, moving each to the side.

Spy Make the sign for *wolf.*

Superiority Hold both hands in front of the chest, with index fingers pointing up, the other fingers closed and palms facing the person addressed. One hand should be held higher than the other, to convey the idea of superiority. To indicate a great degree of superiority, or if what is being judged inferior is large in number, place the right index finger under the extended thumb and fingers of the left hand.

Tomb Make the signs for *dead* and *to dig.*

Treaty If it is between two clans or two tribes, make the signs for *much, smoke* and *handshake.* If it is with the white man, make the signs for *handshake* and *white.*

War Clench both fists at your sides at waist level. Then move them up and forward.

War dance Make the signs for *war* and *dance.*

Wounded, wound With the index finger of the right hand, touch the chest just above the heart.

to strike

to die, death (1)

to die, death (2)

Crow horseman on the warpath.
His long tresses were often a hairpiece. The Indian had a rather special concept of war. He codified and ranked a whole range of exploits: to wound an enemy barehanded or with a score stick carried the greatest honor. Inter-tribal ritual wars were carried out almost like a game. Most of the time they consisted of raids by small bands of warriors whose object was to capture the horses of an enemy tribe. Fully drawn-up battles were, in fact, the exception.

The ballgame of the Indians was in part the ancestor of modern baseball. It was very popular and very violent. It was played between rival tribes and could bring together as many as 600 players on a single field. All the conditions existed for melées of epic proportions.

The game would begin with a dance with the women singing and the men hitting their rackets together in mock play. Then the game started. The ball, a sacred object, was never to be touched with the hands. The game ended when 100 goals had been scored. In the course of the game, which was incredibly violent, many were wounded and sometimes some were even killed. On these occasions, naturally, there was very heavy betting.

Trading and Palavering

to Abandon Hold both hands closed in front of the chest. Then move them forward and downwards, opening them one after the other.

Absent Make in succession the signs for *seated* and *not*.

Abundance Make the sign for *much*.

to Abuse, to misuse Hold the right hand in front of the face, with the thumb extending towards the mouth, the index finger touching the nose, and the other fingers closed. Slowly move the hand away from the face and towards the person addressed. Repeat this several times.

Accord, agreement If it is an accord between two tribes, make the signs for *to do, smoke* and *handshake*. If it is an agreement with Palefaces, do the signs for *handshake* and *Paleface*.

to Add Place the hands, held open at chest level, against one another, the right one on top with palm down, the left hand with palm up. Then slowly lift the hands, taking care to keep them together, to a height of about 4 inches (10 cm). Repeat this gesture several times.

Agent Make the signs for *Paleface, chief, to give* and *food*.

Aid, help (to ask for) Make the signs for *work* and *together*.

Alone, sole Hold the right hand at neck level and point the index finger towards the sky. Then move the hand towards the left in an undulating up-and-down movement.

And Make the sign for *together*.

Another Place the right palm on the left side of the chest. Bring the hand up, then move it back to the side and hold it there for a moment, motionless.

Apart Make the sign for *separate*.

As, like Make the sign for *equal*.

to Attempt, to try Make the signs for *must* and *to push*.

Attention Make the sign for *question*.

Bad Luck Make the signs for *medicine* and *bad*.

to abandon (1)

to abandon (2)

to abuse, misuse

to add (1)

to add (2)

goodbye

exchange (1)

exchange (2)

to explain

Basket Make the sign for *kettle,* then wiggle the fingers to suggest the action of basket-weaving.

to Bet If the betting involves cards, the sign is executed by pretending to put two coins or chips on a table.

to Be unaware of Make the sign for *to know,* then open the hand and bring it towards the right. Finish with the sign for *not.*

Brand, mark With the thumb and index finger of either hand, make a circle; the other fingers remain closed. Then place the circle thus formed against the shoulder if referring to a brand on the shoulder, or against the hip if it is a brand on the rump.

But Make the sign for *perhaps.*

to Buy Make the signs for *money* and *to exchange.*

By oneself Hold the right hand in front of the chest on the right side. With a movement of the wrist, guide the right hand towards the left and in front of the body, shaking the hand two or three times. When this sign precedes the giving of a present, it means that nothing is expected in return. This sign also means *solitude, liberty* and *alone.*

Cannot Raise the right hand obliquely a short distance in front of the chest. Point the right index finger towards the middle of your left side. Then move the right index finger forward until it comes into contact with the palm of the left hand. In anticipation of this contact the left hand has been vertically turned towards the chest. Finally, pull the right index finger briskly back.

Certain Make the signs for *me, know* and *good.*

to Challenge Hold the right hand at chest level and place the right thumb between the right index and middle fingers. Then quickly move the hand towards the person addressed.

Coffee Hold the left hand palm up against the chest, then lower it to waist level. Close the right hand and bring it up a short distance from the left hand. Then make circles with the right hand, as though you are grinding coffee beans.

Comrade, companion Make the signs for *friend* and *equal.*

much

to challenge

to understand

to defame, to slander (1)

to defame, to slander (2)

how much

to Conduct business, to negotiate Hold both forearms raised, hands closed, index fingers pointing up. Then lower the hands together, passing them in front of the chest.

Congress First make the signs for *house, important, Paleface* and *chief.* Then make the sign for *to bring,* repeating it in several different directions. Finish with the signs for *to sit down* and *council.*

to Consider Make the sign for *perhaps.*

Trading and Palavering

effort

to wrap

impossible

to attempt, to try

evidently

it must

people

impossible

sign language

to miss, to lack

to lie (1)

to lie (2)

Decision Hold the left hand open, palm up. Place the right hand vertically above the left, moving it up from the side of the waist rapidly.

to Defame, to slander Hold the right hand at mouth level, index and middle fingers extended. Then move the hand towards the person addressed.

to Distribute Move the right hand towards the left side, then to the right side, making the gesture of giving something. Return hand to its original position and repeat.

Dollar Make the sign for *money* and then the sign for *one*.

Effort Same sign as *to push:* Place both hands, closed, on either side of the chest. Then move them forward a few inches, slowly, as though making an effort.

End Hold the left hand vertically on the left side of chest, fingers held together and pointing up. Then rapidly lower the right hand, held open, letting it graze the tips of the left fingers in passing.

Evidently Raise the right hand in front of the right side, fingers pointing forward. By moving the wrist, guide the right hand to the left and in front of the body, shaking it two or three times. When preceded by this sign, the bestowing of a gift has no strings attached.

to Exchange Place both hands at shoulder level, index fingers pointing up. Lower the hands and pass one hand in front of the other, describing a quarter circle.

to Explain Hold the right hand open, at mouth level, with palm up and fingers spread. Then, keeping the wrist stationary, pivot the hand to the right.

Fame, renown If you wish to pay the finest compliment to an Indian, it is enough to tell him that he is *brave* and that he behaves like a *chief*. Therefore make the appropriate signs.

Farm Make the signs for *maize* and *work*.

Finished, accomplished Make the sign for *end*.

Flour Hold the right hand at chest level and rub the tips of the fingers with the thumb. Show something white and finish with the sign for *bread*.

Foodstuffs Make the sign for *to eat*.

Give me Extend the right hand forward in a gesture of asking for something. Then bring it towards the shoulder.

Goodbye Make the sign for *future*.

He, him (emphatic) Point the right index finger in the direction of the person referred to.

Heap, pile Hold the two hands apart at waist level, palms facing and fingers spread. Then bring the hands together until they meet in the middle at shoulder level, describing a curve as you raise them.

How much With fingers outstretched and palm down, hold the left hand at neck level at a 45° angle towards the right hand, which is held slightly forward of the left. Then, with the index finger of the right hand, tap the left little finger, then the other left fingers. As each finger is touched, it curls under.

Impossible Make the sign for *cannot*.

Intelligence, wit Touch the forehead with the right index and middle fingers.

Interpreter Make the signs for *he, to speak, Paleface* and (again) *to speak*.

to Interrogate Make the sign for *to question*.

It must Make the sign for *to push*.

to Know Hold the right hand on the right side of the chest at the level of the heart, with thumb and index finger extended. Then move the hand slightly upwards and outwards. With a wrist movement pivot the hand until the palm is turned up, the thumb and index finger still extended and the other fingers closed. At this point the thumb should be pointing up and the index finger pointing to the left.

Law Make the sign for *truth*.

mine

me, myself

thank you

to Lie (to have two tongues) Hold the right hand on the right side of the mouth, with index and middle fingers extended and pointing towards the left.

Lost Make the sign for *to hide*.

Me, myself Point to yourself with either the right or left hand, fingers closed and thumb aimed towards your chest.

Memory Make the signs for *heart* and *to know*.

to Miss, to lack Make the sign for *poor*.

Mistake, fault Hold both hands open, parallel to one another, palms facing. Then slide the right hand under the left as though hiding something there.

Money Hold the right hand slightly in front of the chest and form an incomplete circle with the thumb and index finger. The other fingers remain closed.

Much Make the sign for *big*.

yes

partner

Not Make the sign for *cannot*.

Not to speak First make the sign for *not*. Then clench the right fingers and bring them up to the mouth. Open and close the fingers two or three times.

Oath Formerly the signs used to designate this word were numerous. Many tribes pointed to the highest heavens, then to the earth. Today, they raise the right hand in the way the Palefaces do when they are taking an oath.

Part If something cut in two is involved, make the sign for *half*. If further divisions are involved, indicate this accordingly.

Partner Simply make the sign for *brother*. The word partner does not exist in the Indian vocabulary. When Indians have a high regard for someone, they consider him a *friend* or *brother*.

People Hold both hands at chest level, index fingers extended upwards, the tips of the thumbs touching, the other fingers closed. Then move each hand to its own side. Some tribes place both hands on the chest with the backs of the hands facing outwards.

Perhaps This sign means "two hearts." Point to your heart with the index and middle fingers of the right hand, keeping the other fingers closed. Then twist the right hand, alternately touching the heart with the index and middle fingers, thus expressing doubt.

Please Hold the right hand against the chest. Move it down slowly towards the ground, palm up. Done in reverse, this sign means *give me*.

Possession, property Make the sign for *mine*.

Probably Place the right hand on the heart, with the index and middle fingers extended and slightly spread apart. With a movement of the forearm, guide the hand towards the right, then forward, the back of the hand facing the person addressed. If there is considerable doubt, shake or turn the hand on completing the sign.

Quarrel, dispute Raise the hands to neck level and hold them about 8 inches (20 cm) apart, index fingers pointing up, the other fingers closed. Then alternately move the right hand to the right and the left hand to the left. Repeat this several times.

to bet

to think

perhaps

to Read Make the signs for *book* and *to see*.

to Recall, remember Make the signs for *heart* and *to know*.

to Remain Make the sign for *to sit down*.

to Remember Point the left index finger downwards and grasp it with the right hand. The left elbow should be at shoulder level and the arm stretched horizontally.

to Repeat Make the sign for *often*.

to Retake, recapture Extend the left hand, open, in front of you, palm forward, fingers pointing up. Place the right hand against the right side of the chest, index finger pointing up, the other fingers closed. Then move it towards the left hand until the two hands touch.

to Sell Make the sign for *exchange*.

She, her (emphatic) Point the right index finger in the direction of the person referred to.

Sign language Cross the wrists, the right wrist over the left one, at lower chest level. The hands are open and palms are down. Then make the sign for *to speak*.

Silence Place the right fingertips on the mouth, then nod the head slightly forward.

Similar (referring to two tribes that resemble each other) Make the signs for *face* and *equal*.

to Speak If a short conversation is involved, one

possession, property

quarrel, dispute

to retake, recapture

in which one person is speaking to another, press the nail of the right index finger against the right thumb, extending the other fingers forward. Raise your hand slightly and point the index finger. If a larger gathering is involved—a meeting of several people or a powwow—lift the right hand, palm up, fingers extended and spread to a point in front of the mouth. Then move the hand slightly. Repeat the gesture for both types of conversation.

Speak, I am about to   First point to yourself with your right index finger. Then close your hand and place it near your mouth. Then open and close the fingers several times.

Standing   Hold the right hand on the right side, a little above the shoulder, with the index finger pointing up.

Store, shop   Make the signs for *house* and *commerce*.

to Swindle   Make the signs for *to lie* and *to steal*.

Telephone   With the fingertips slightly bent, bring your right hand to your ear. Move your left index finger towards the right palm to symbolize the wire. Finish with the sign for *to speak*. To the Indians, it is a question of speaking through a wire.

Tell me   Hold the open right hand 4 inches (10 cm) in front of the mouth, palm facing the mouth. Then very quickly bring it close to the face.

Thank you   Extend both open hands, palms down, in a forward direction. Then lower them as far as possible.

Theirs   Point with the right index finger to the persons in question.

They (emphatic)   Make the sign for *all*.

to Think   Hold the right hand firmly against the chest, with the index finger pointing forward at the level of the heart and the other fingers closed. Turn the hand horizontally a little to the front and to the left. Finish by turning the palm towards the ground.

To, at   Extend the left hand, palm up, fingers together. Then place the tips of the right fingers on top of the left fingers in such a way that the left fingers appear to be extensions of the right ones.

alone, sole

silence

end, to end

another

to Trade   Make the sign for *exchange*.

Truth, true   Hold the right hand in front of the chin, palm down, index finger extended, the other fingers closed.

to Understand   Make the sign for *to know*.

Well?   Make the sign for *to question*. Then turn up the right hand very slowly and raise both hands to a point close to the chest, with the index fingers extended.

to Wish   Turn to the side and close your left hand, leaving the index finger only partly curled. Bring the hand to the mouth and touch the lips, then firmly lower the hand towards the ground. This sign is also used to mean *energy* and *I wish*.

to Wrap   Hold the left hand in front of the body, palm down, fingers together. Tap the upper side of the left hand with the right fingertips, then the underside of it. Then reverse the gesture: tap the upper side and then the underside of the right hand with the left fingertips.

Yes   Place the back of the right hand on the right side of the chest near the shoulder. The index finger is extended; the other fingers are closed, the thumb resting on the middle finger. Move the hand slightly to the left, at the same time closing the index finger over the thumb.

You   Point the right index finger towards the person referred to.

Your   Make the sign for *you* and then the one for *possession*.

truth, true

Picture Writing

The picture writing used by the Indians was the written form of sign language. Each sign represented a word (object, thing, living being, idea) but never a letter.

Like the language of gesture, picture writing had many signs that had become conventional. Picture writing was especially well developed among the Sioux (the Teton-Dakota in particular) and the Kiowa. In these tribes, the most important deeds of the year were told pictographically on a sort of bison-hide calendar. Some of the facts thus recorded may seem of little interest to us compared to some of the historical events of the same period—events well known to us concerning a particular tribe, but not considered worth mentioning by that tribe. This difference in emphasis reflected the different values of the Indians and the Palefaces. The Indians reported, "the year when the smallpox epidemic wiped out a great many people," or "the year they saw the first white man," but did not record the death of General Custer, which they avoided boasting about for fear of reprisals.

Pictographic symbols were also used on blankets, which became sartorial autobiographies in which the valiant warriors draped themselves. The tepees were also decorated with them, of course, and in this ornate form became famous throughout the world.

Examples of pictographic signs shown on page 69.

Calendars. The best known pictographic record (calendar) is that of Lone Dog, covering a period between 1800 and 1870.

Chronology. 1. Time (three years). **2.** 1801-1802. Year in which many Indians died of smallpox. **3.** 1804-1805. The Dakotas have a pipe-smoking and dance ritual and, unified, go off to war. **4.** 1819-1820. Construction of a second trading post at Fort Pierre by Louis La Conte. **5.** 1821-1822. Sighting of a meteor. **6.** 1832-1833. Lone Horn breaks his leg. **7.** 1836-1837. The father of the chief of the Two Kettles Band dies of indigestion after eating bison (the sign is the conventional one for *bison*). **8.** 1839-1840. The Dakotas destroy an entire village of Shoshones. **9.** 1845-1846. Abundance of bisons. **10.** 1849-1850. The Crows steal 800 horses from the Brule Sioux. **11.** 1851-1852. Peace with the Crows. **12.** 1855-1856. Peace with General Harney. **13.** 1856-1857. Four Horns does the peace pipe dance and is acknowledged as a medicine man. He will become famous in a few years under the name of Sitting Bull. **14.** 1869-1870. Eclipse of the sun (August 7, 1869). **15.** 1870-1871. The Dakotas close in on the Crows in the Black Hills and lose fourteen of their men. **16.** 1814-1815. The Dakotas kill an Arapaho in his lodge (tepee). **17.** 1861-1862. Bisons are so abundant that they leave tracks near the tepees.

Tribal Designations. 18. Battle between Dakotas (a) and Crows (b). **19.** Cheyenne ("Finger Cutter"). **20.** Mandan. **21.** Cheyenne. The cross, symbol of the Cheyenne.

Exploits and Marks. 22. Thefts of horses: hoof painted on blankets. **23.** Escaped from the enemy by hiding behind a hillock. **24.** First to wound the enemy (Hidatsa). **25.** The fourth. **26.** The same meaning as 25. **27.** Wounded the fourth, took his scalp and his gun (Hidatsa). **28.** Scalped his enemy. **29.** Killed.

The Supernatural. 30. Medicine. **31.** Medicine bison. **32.** Making medicine.

Daily Life. 33. Punishing an adulterer. **34.** Suicide. **35.** Leader of a war party.

Historic Events. 36. Trader. **37.** 4-point blanket. **38.** Mexican blanket. **39.** Capture of a wagon. **40.** Encircled by the enemy.

Abstract Ideas. 41. Old. **42.** Bad. **43.** Sickness. **44.** High. **45.** Fasting. **46.** Thin. **47.** Small. **48.** Much. **49.** Prisoner. **50.** Prisoner. **51.** Union. **52.** Union. **53.** Snow. **54.** Coward.

Conventional. 55. Peace (Dakotas, Pawnees). **56.** War (Cheyennes, Dakotas, 1834-1835). **57.** Council. **58.** Abundance. **59.** Maize. **60.** Capture of a horse. **61.** Killed. **62.** Killed a bear. **63.** Shot at with bullets. **64.** Killed by an arrow. **65.** Speech, conversation.

Habitation. 66. House (tepee), see No. 8 and No. 17. **67.** Meteors. **68.** Prayer. **69.** Beaver. **70.** Mark of Crazy Horse.

Speech through signs and pictographs.
1. to listen. **2.** to see. **3.** to speak. **4.** peace.

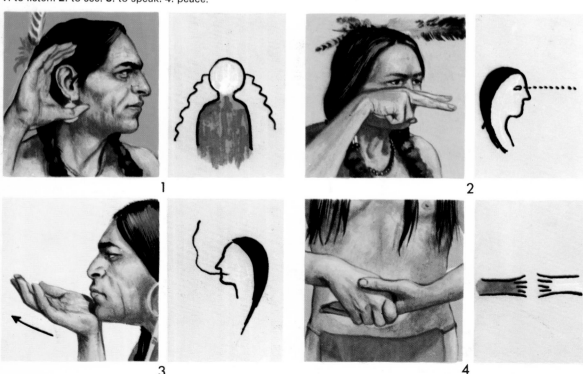

1   2

3   4

A History of War

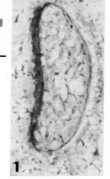

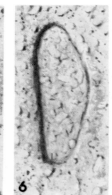

as told to us by pictographs on a Blackfoot tepee

1. Bear Chief, on foot, is surprised by Assiniboins, but succeeds in escaping them. **2.** Double Runner lets four horses escape. **3.** Double Runner captures a Gros Ventre child. **4.** Double Runner and one of his warriors encounter and kill two Gros Ventres. **5.** As a child, he takes the war bonnet of a Gros Ventre and marks up a score. **6.** Grown up, he fights two Crows and seizes the gun of one of them. **7.** Head of a war party, he encounters five Flatheads hidden in a gully and kills them. **8.** A Cree has hidden in a hole covered with cherry branches, but Double Runner finds him. **9.** Double Runner kills the Cree, while the horses of the Blackfeet run away. **10.** Double Runner, carrying his medicine pipe, takes the bow away from a Gros Ventre and kills him. **11.** Double Runner steals a shield and a horse from in front of a Crow tepee. **12.** He kills two Gros Ventres and takes their arms. **13.** He captures a Gros Ventre woman and child. **14.** He brings back four mules from a raid.

Moccasin Prints

1. Crow

2. Teton Sioux

3. Cheyenne

4. Arapaho

5. Pawnee

6. Kiowa

Trail and Exploit Marks

The sun was setting slowly, casting beautiful colors upon the clouds far off on the horizon. A light, both soft and sad, bathed the empty prairie, transfixed in the silence that precedes the shadows of dusk.

Brave Bear restrained his high-strung mustang with a firm hand as he proceeded watchfully at a slow trot. Suddenly he saw the sign he was looking for. He fixed his eyes on a white spot, still far off, on the edge of the trail. Shortly, as he got nearer, his broad, copper-colored face lit up with a smile. Finally, he stopped his horse. At his feet, arranged in a semi-circle and facing the stream, were fifteen bison skulls. In the middle was another skull, painted with thirty-eight scarlet stripes, and beside this five sticks were driven into the ground, each crowned with a tuft of horsehair. Brave Bear could thus read the eyewitness account of a drama:

"Thirty-eight Cheyenne carried out a successful raid against a Pawnee village of fifteen earthen huts. They took five scalps and went home after fording the river." His fellow tribesmen had achieved a great victory, but the Pawnee would one day avenge this bloodshed.

This is how the Cheyenne communicated using trail signs. A white man, of course, would only have seen some bones arranged in a bizarre fashion, and it would have meant little or nothing to him.

SMOKE SIGNALS

In order to communicate over great distances, the Indians had recourse to visual signals achieved with mirrors obtained from the whites, or to smoke signals, which, on many an occasion, caused pangs of fear to spread in pioneer wagon trains on their way to conquer the West. To make smoke signals they began by lighting a fire of damp grass under a pyramid of brush. The fire would quickly release a dense column of smoke. All that had to be done then was alternately cover the pyramid of branches with a blanket and remove the blanket, following a certain rhythm, to produce, according to a precise code, spirals of smoke of different sizes at different intervals. Thus it amounted to a sort of Morse alphabet, the key to which we do not have, unfortunately. What we do know is very limited: one cloud – be careful! two clouds – all is well, three clouds or three fires in a row – help!

At night the Indians used blazing arrows, which they shot in the air to different heights. Lastly were the drums, which announced great events, and whose rolls reverberated across the prairie from tribe to tribe.

TRAIL SIGNS

A bunch of grass tied in a bunch will give, according to its freshness, the date on which those who made it passed that way. Two or three stones piled on top of one another might constitute a warning or indicate a direction. Several branches stuck in the soil might mean as many days as there are branches. The Indians were experts in the art of making nature speak. Some examples appear on the right.

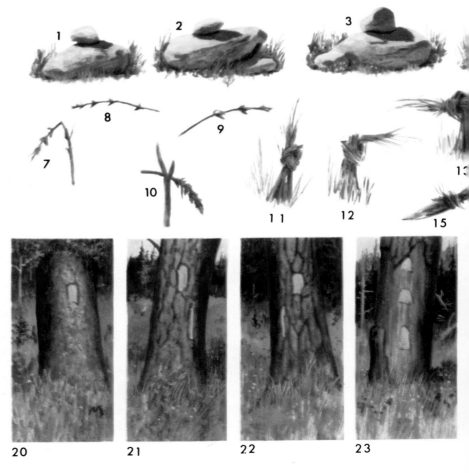

Trail signs (made according to available natural materials). **1-7-11** and **20**, this is the way. **2-8-12** and **21**, turn right. **3-9-13** and **22**, turn left. **4-10-14** and **23**, important notice. **5.** We camped here because one of us was sick (this sign stems from the use of steam baths—the pile of pebbles are the remains of stones heated white hot, on which cold water was poured, instantly creating invigorating steam). **6.** Water in this direction. **15.** Watch out! Danger! **16.** Not very far from here. **17.** A four-days' march away. **18.** We have gone bear hunting in this direction. **19.** Plenty of game but we are short of ammunition. **24.** River full of fish. **25.** We're starving. Help!

Among the Mandans of the upper Missouri River a bundle of sticks was left during the night in front of the hut of a debtor to remind him discreetly of his debt.

Generally, a tomahawk or arrow painted red meant war. A broken arrow, placed in full view across the trail meant that one must not go any farther or face the consequences.

THE LANGUAGE OF FEATHERS

The language of feathers was used chiefly by the Plains Indians as a means of parading their achievements. Here are some examples.
Among the Hidatsas. 1. Eagle feather decorated with a tuft of horse hair dyed red: was the first to strike and kill the enemy. **2.** Was wounded in battle. **3.** Second to wound the enemy. **4.** The third. **5.** The fourth.
Among the Dakota-Sioux. 6. Killed one enemy. **7.** Killed three of them. **8.** Cut his throat and scalped him. **9.** Cut his throat only. The first coup (score) is indicated by an eagle feather stuck vertically into the hair, the second by a feather placed horizontally in the hair. **10.** Third to wound the enemy. **11.** The fourth . . . **12.** Was wounded several times. **13.** The fifth . . . **14.** The bands on the shaft of the feather indicate the number of enemies killed. Made of porcupine quill, each band stands for one enemy.

THE LANGUAGE OF BLANKETS

Among the Omahas, the manner in which the blanket was draped indicated various conditions. **A.** The ardor of youth. **B.** Ready to run. **C.** Age—the way the blanket is worn indicates the weakness of old age. At the tribal council? **D.** State of rage. **E.** Speech: the chief is ready to address the Council of the Tribe. **F.** Hesitation.
The blanket, when removed from the body, was also used to make signals from a distance. To swing it unfolded over the head meant a discovery. Rolled up and held up by both ends, in the shape of bison horns, it meant bisons. To give an alarm, a blanket was thrown into the air several times.

To pay court to the girl of his dreams, a young Indian would hide his face behind his blanket at night and go play the flute near the tepee of his beloved. If he was accepted, the young girl would paint her cheeks red with cinnabar.

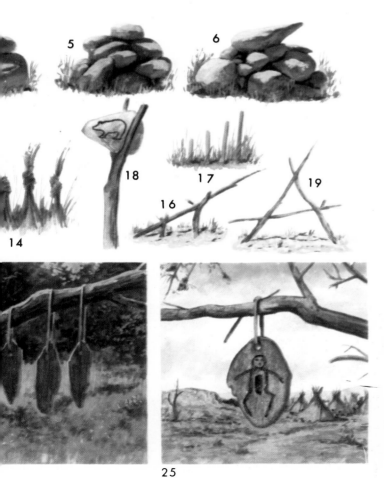

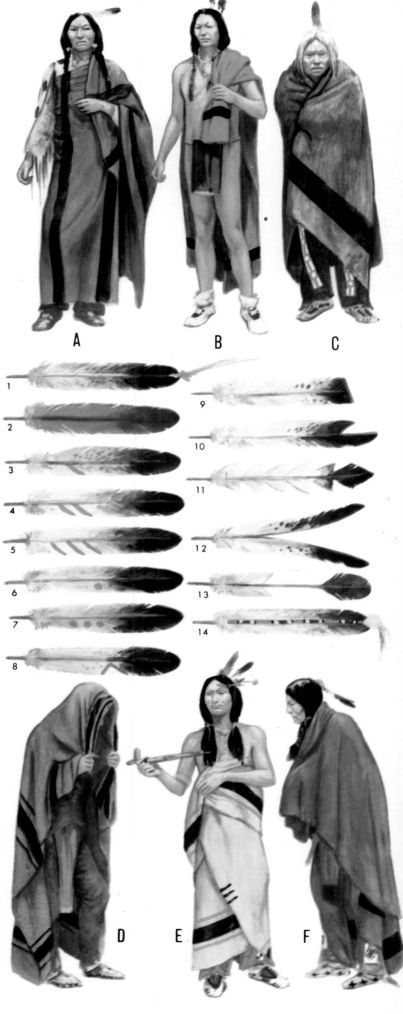

25

Exploits of
Mato Topa the Magnificent

Mato Topa (Four Bears), the illustrious Mandan warrior with the bear claw necklace, was given his name by his Assiniboin enemies, for he displayed an astonishing strength in combat.

One day, following a skirmish with the Arikara, Mato Topa discovered his brother on the ground impaled by the spear of a redoubtable enemy – Won ga tap. He wept for a long time. Then, in front of the assembled tribe, he took an oath to avenge his brother by killing his murderer with the same lance that had killed him. To that end, he took possession of the gloomy weapon, left the village and proceeded 190 miles (300 km) on foot, hiding by day, travelling by night, subsisting on a little maize.

When he reached the Arikara village, he entered it in disguise, located the hut of his enemy and at nightfall peeked inside it through a crack between two boards. Won ga tap had just gone to bed after smoking a final pipe. Without hesitating, Mato Topa entered and sat down by the still-glowing hearth. He helped himself to meat, and even went so far as to take the pipe and tobacco of Won ga tap for a smoke. He knew very well that his presence would not surprise anyone, for, according to the customs of these tribes, whoever was hungry could enter anyone's hut to refresh himself. The law of hospitality was sacred.

Mato Topa gently poked the dying embers in order to get a better view of his enemy's bed. Then he suddenly leaped up and with a mortal blow plunged the spear into the heart of Won ga tap. Uttering a fearsome war cry, he took his scalp and, quick as lightning, disappeared into the night before the alarm was given.

His return to the village was triumphal. The blood debt had been paid.

Several years earlier when Mato Topa was younger, a Cheyenne war party of fifty braves attacked the Mandan village. Although the assault was fierce, the attackers were repulsed and put to flight. Mato Topa, leading fifty braves, took off on a two-day pursuit of the enemy. The next morning, the Mandan came within sight of the Cheyenne. Realizing that they were outnumbered, the Mandan were reluctant to engage in combat and even began to retreat.

On seeing this, Mato Topa leaped from his horse, thrust his spear into the edge of his scarlet robe and shouted to his men, "You may well desert me, but it will not be said that Mato Topa is a coward. I shall fight alone against them all, if I have to." The Cheyenne chief, understanding the situation and struck with admiration for the valor and boldness of his adversary, rode up at a slow trot, and called, "Who is this brave who defies us thus?"

"I am Mato Topa, second ranking chief of the Mandan and brave among the braves."

"I have often heard you spoken of as a noble warrior. Your renown is great. Do you agree to do battle with me?"

"Is he who speaks to me a Cheyenne chief?"

"I am a chief among the Cheyenne! See my many scalps and my fine eagle feathers. They will tell you of my deeds."

"Good," answered Mato Topa. "I see that you are a brave. . . ." The Cheyenne and the Mandan formed a circle round their two champions and the fight to the death began. One might have described them as two eagles after their prey. Bending their bows, they vigorously released arrow after arrow. One arrow pierced the heart of Mato Topa's mustang. Unhorsed, the Mandan got up immediately, ready to ward off blows. The Cheyenne too dismounted, brandishing his scalping knife.

The Mandan went for his own knife, but the sheath was empty. A struggle began for possession of the Cheyenne's knife. Mato Topa was wounded several times. The blood poured from his wounds. Finally, in a supreme effort, he succeeded in throwing his enemy to the ground, then took the knife away from him and stabbed him in the chest. Then he let out his awesome war cry. He had won. Before the hypnotized crowd, Mato Topa proudly waved a bloody scalp. A deathly silence followed a tumult of cries, and then the Cheyenne, demoralized, turned back.

Thus the hero of the Mandan added another exploit to the many that the elders were already telling about during the long winter vigils.

This illustrious chief, a great friend of George Catlin, let himself waste away from grief after the death of his wife and children in the terrible smallpox epidemic of 1837 that devastated the noble Mandan tribe.

Here is what George Catlin wrote in 1832, as a commentary on the portrait he painted, and which is reproduced on the opposite page: "Mah-to-toh-pa (Four Bears), second ranking chief of the Mandans, is the most popular and most esteemed man of his tribe. He is a man of liberty, generosity, elegance, and is noble in his deportment. He is handsome and brave. He usually wears a bison-hide tunic on which is painted the history of his exploits, a history so packed that it could fill an entire book. He is one of the most extraordinary Indians that I have known."

Body Paint, Called War Paint

The Indians, who had an innate sense of color and decoration, painted their faces, originally at least, to protect themselves from the wind, the sun, the snow and especially from insect bites.

This paint, wrongly called "war paint," did not always have a direct connection with warfare. It was, above all, personal painting, "medicine" for war, for the hunt, and to indicate the rank and merits of the wearer, as well as for numerous religious ceremonies. The Indian was in fact a very religious being, especially attracted to the spirit world.

FACIAL PAINT

Blackfeet. 1. Stu-Mick-O-Sucks, high chief of the Bloods. His paint was intended to help him be victorious over his enemies. **2.** Pe-Toh-Pee-Kiss, chief of the Piegans. The horns symbolize his prowess in "medicine." **3.** Mehskeme-Sukahs, chief of the Blackfeet. **4.** Blackfoot chief. **5.** Member of the Front Tail Society (Blackfoot). **6.** Medicine man of the Sundance.
Plains Crees. 7. Bro-Cas-Sie. **8.** Cree woman with tattoos.
Mandans. 9. O-Kee-Hee-De, the Evil Spirit, who during the Male Bison Dance, mimes the mating ritual of the bisons. **10.** Paint for the "last race."
Arikaras. 11. Stan-au Pat, chief of the Arikaras.
Hidatsa (Minitare). 12. The paint indicates that the wearer has killed an enemy barehanded.
Sioux-Teton Dakota*. 13. Oglala chief of the Bad Arrow Point band with his war paint. **14.** Miniconjou chief. His paint shows that he returned from war with many scalps and that he was wounded in the forehead (red spot). The little stick in his hair means that he killed an enemy with a gun. **15.** Son-ka, Teton chief of the Bad Arrow Point band. **16.** War paint of the Oglala chief, Crazy Horse. His face paint represents the numerous coups he has scored against enemies. **17.** Paint signifying war and vengeance. **18.** Teton woman in festival paint.
Assiniboins. 19. Member of the Bear Cult Society.
Arapaho. 20. Black Man—his paint symbolizes speed and power. The semi-circle represents the vault of the heavens from which lightning emanates.
Cheyenne. 21. Tis-See-Woo-Na-Tis, a Cheyenne woman. **22.** Cheyenne warrior. **23.** Member of the Wolf Warrior Society.
Kiowa. 24. Woman. Paint is for the victorious return of the warriors.
Pawnee. 25. La-Doo-Ke-A. His paint symbolizes the Male Bison.
Omaha. 26. Om-pa-Ton-ga, with a head-dress of porcupine quills dyed red. **27.** Paint indicating that the fire of vengeance in his heart is burned out and that he wishes peace with his soul.
Iowa. 28. Little Wolf. **Kansas. 29.** Man of good sense. **Oto. 30.** No-way-Ke-sug-ga.

---

* The Western Sioux or Teton-Dakotas included the Brules, the Sans-Arcs the Blackfoot Sioux (Siha-Sapa), the Miniconjous, the Two Kettles, the Oglalas and the Hunkpapas.

(Below, top)
Paint of the Okeepa of the Mandans. Male Bison dance, preceding the initiation ceremony for young Mandans. Left to right: Male Bison, Night, Day (the white stripes stand for the phantoms chased by the morning light), the Snake.

(Below, bottom)
Paint for the Sundance (Arapaho, Cheyenne). The most important religious ceremony, common to all the Plains Tribes. It was celebrated following a vow made during great danger.

War Dance (by George Catlin)

Before leaving on an expedition against an enemy village, the warriors decorated their bodies with paint and danced in order to ask Wakan Tanka (the Great Spirit in Sioux) for strength and courage. To the mournful sound of the drums, the dancers assumed menacing attitudes and frantically brandished their war clubs and spears, simulating the combat that they were about to engage in and uttering terrifying war cries.

Sioux horsemen returning from a successful raid

The blue spots on the face of the rider in the middle indicate numerous coups against enemies. His hair is adorned, apart from a scalp lock, with two eagle feathers. One tells that he was the first to wound and kill an enemy. The other, painted red, tells that he was wounded in an earlier battle. On his left side, an old wound is surrounded by a black circle, from which sunbeams radiate (this a prayer that the heat of the sun come to cure him). On his arms and legs are painted red lines (his coups) and yellow ones (the number of horses he has stolen). In his left hand, he proudly holds the emblem of the Dog Soldiers Society, a military elite, which gives him the rank of second in command of this war party.

His mount is painted to record his master's exploits: the red lines on the nose indicate coups. The circle around the eye is intended to aid the horse's eyesight. On the breast, a red hand (killed an enemy barehanded), three horseshoes (number of horses stolen), on the hind legs, coups. On the hindquarters, the blue lines stand for membership in a military society. The tail of the mustang is knotted for a military expedition.

The horseman on the right is an Oglala Sioux war chief. His men followed him because he was the bravest and also the luckiest. He is painted, as is his horse, with the marks of his society, and he holds his standard of command and his war shield, powerful medicine which was thought to ward off mortal blows delivered by the enemy.

The horseman on the left is a brave in war paint. He holds in one hand his coup (score) stick and in the other the reins of his pony, who bears symbols of the lightning that gives him speed and strength.

Index

The words in boldface correspond to the signs that are both illustrated by a photograph and described in the text, while the lightface indicates only those signs described in the text. The page numbers in boldface indicate the pages of the photographs, while the lightface numbers refer to the text entries.

80